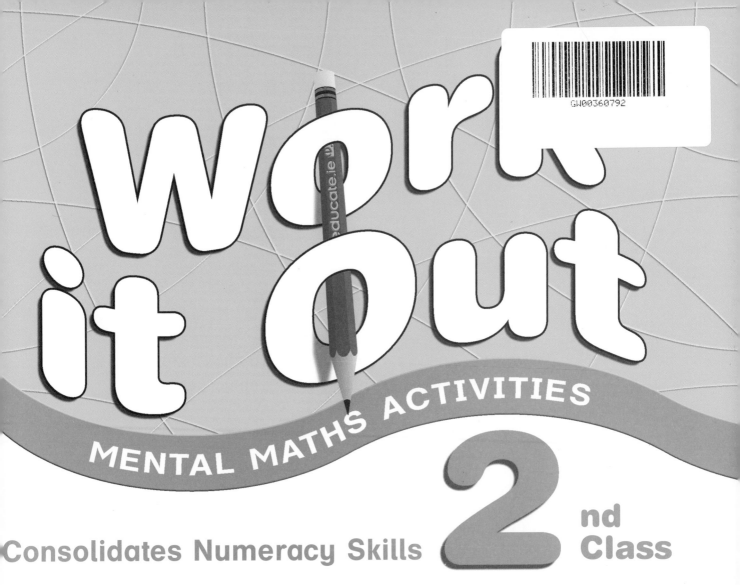

Work it Out

MENTAL MATHS ACTIVITIES

Consolidates Numeracy Skills

2 nd Class

Sue Synnott

educate.ie

Editor: Ciara McNee
Design and layout: Philip Ryan Graphic Design
Illustrations: Philip Ryan Graphic Design

© 2013 Educate.ie, Castleisland, County Kerry, Ireland

ISBN: 978-1-909376-13-7

Printed in Ireland by Walsh Colour Print, Castleisland, County Kerry.
Freephone 1800 613 111

INTRODUCTION

Work it Out is a programme of six Mental Maths Activity Books for 1st to 6th Class. The series is in line with the strands and strand units of the Revised Primary School Curriculum.

Each book is based on the 30 weeks of the school year, with daily mental exercises. The questions are varied and they increase in complexity as the weeks progress.

The Monday to Thursday exercises include a Tables Section, plus 10 other questions. The Friday Tests comprise 10 multiple choice questions broadly based on the previous days' questions.

The daily mental exercises and Friday Tests provide for self-assessment and assessment of learning.

Answers are available on www.educate.ie.

CONTENTS

TABLES

1. $1 + 7 =$ ☐
2. $1 + 2 =$ ☐
3. $1 + 5 =$ ☐
4. $1 + 4 =$ ☐
5. $1 + 6 =$ ☐

6.  It is ☐ o'clock.

7. $\frac{1}{2}$ of 4 is ☐ . 〜〜〜〜〜〜

8. $7 +$ ☐ $= 10$

9. What number comes next?

   2, 4, 6, 8, ☐

10. Add 4 to 9. ☐

11. Two stools have ☐ legs.

12. Laura has 10 🍬. Kim has 5 less. How many sweets has Kim? ☐

13. Name this shape. ◯ _____

14.  How much? ☐ c

15. Ring the even numbers.

    2   3   4   5   6

😞 ☐   😐 ☐   🙂 ☐   Score ◯ 15

Work it out.

1. ☐ $+ 1 = 10$
2. ☐ $+ 1 = 9$
3. ☐ $+ 1 = 8$
4. ☐ $+ 1 = 3$
5. ☐ $+ 1 = 1$
6. ☐ $+ 1 = 11$
7. ☐ $+ 1 = 10$
8. ☐ $+ 1 = 5$
9. ☐ $+ 1 = 3$
10. ☐ $+ 1 = 4$
11. $1 +$ ☐ $= 12$

12. $1 +$ ☐ $= 5$
13. $1 +$ ☐ $= 11$
14. $1 +$ ☐ $= 7$
15. $1 +$ ☐ $= 6$
16. $1 +$ ☐ $= 12$
17. $1 +$ ☐ $= 2$
18. $1 +$ ☐ $= 9$
19. $1 +$ ☐ $= 7$
20. $1 +$ ☐ $= 8$

😞 ☐   😐 ☐   🙂 ☐   Score ◯ 20

WEDNESDAY – WEEK 1

TABLES

1. $1 + \boxed{} = 7$

2. $1 + \boxed{} = 1$

3. $0 + 1 = \boxed{}$

4. $\boxed{} + 1 = 11$

5. $1 + 4 = \boxed{}$

6. Colour half.

7.  Paul has $\boxed{}$ c.

8. Finish the pattern.

△ □ △ ____ ____

9. Two spiders have $\boxed{}$ legs.

10. I am a _____.

11. Tick which holds more.  □

12. $20 - 10 = \boxed{}$

13. The 1st month of the year is _____.

14. Ring the even numbers.

  1   2   3   4   5

15. Show 3 o'clock.

☹ □ 😐 □ ☺ □ **Score** $\frac{}{15}$

Work it out

THURSDAY – WEEK 1

TABLES

1. $3 + 1 = \boxed{}$

2. $1 + 8 = \boxed{}$

3. $9 + 1 = \boxed{}$

4. $1 + \boxed{} = 5$

5. $\boxed{} + 1 = 1$

6. (15c) + (4c) = $\boxed{}$ c

7. Ring the tens digit.   37

8. Write the number before 20. $\boxed{}$

9. Jenna has 9 ▦.

  Alex has 4 crayons more.

  How many has Alex? $\boxed{}$

10. How many days in a week? $\boxed{}$

11. Tick the heavier one.

12. $\frac{1}{2}$ of 8 is $\boxed{}$. ★☆★★ ★☆★☆

13. $10 + \boxed{} = 16$

14. A square has $\boxed{}$ sides.

15.
$$
\begin{array}{r}
35 \\
+\ 20 \\
\hline
\boxed{}
\end{array}
$$

☹ □ 😐 □ ☺ □ **Score** $\frac{}{15}$

Page 66 for Friday Test – Week 1.

TABLES

1. 2 + 5 = 7
2. 2 + 6 = 8
3. 2 + 3 = 5
4. 2 + 9 = 11
5. 2 + 7 = 9

6. There are ☐ months in a year.

7. Colour half.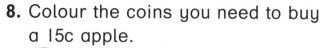

8. Colour the coins you need to buy a 15c apple.

 10c   2c   2c   2c   1c

9. 29 is the number before 30.

10. 25 – 5 = 20

11. Ring the units digit.   2(5)

12. A rectangle has 4 corners.

13. Tick the heavier one.

14. Colour the 1st boy blue.

15. Finish the pattern.
△ ☐ ○ △ ☐ ○ △ ☐ _

 Score ◯ /15

Work it out

---

1. 2 + 9 = 11
2. 7 + 2 = 9
3. ☐ + 2 = 4
4. ☐ + 2 = 10
5. ☐ + 2 = 3
6. ☐ + 2 = 12
7. ☐ + 2 = 8
8. ☐ + 2 = 6
9. ☐ + 2 = 11
10. ☐ + 2 = 7
11. 2 + ☐ = 6

12. 2 + ☐ = 8
13. 2 + ☐ = 5
14. 2 + ☐ = 10
15. ☐ + 2 = 5
16. 2 + ☐ = 7
17. 2 + ☐ = 3
18. 2 + ☐ = 9
19. 2 + ☐ = 2
20. 2 + ☐ = 12

Score ◯ /20

TABLES

1. 2 + 3 = 5
2. 2 + 10 = 12
3. 7 + 2 = 9
4. 8 + 2 = 10
5. 2 + 8 = 10

6. Fill in the missing numbers.

   5, 7, 9, 12, 14

7. Start at 5. Count on 2. Count on 2 again. I am now at 9.

8. = 2 tens 4 units

9. I am a rectangle

10. Paula has 15c. Ian has 6c.
    They have 19 c altogether.

11. 30 + 20 = 40

12. It is 2 o'clock.

13. (3 + 2) + 1 = 6

14.

	5		
4		
3		
2		
1		
	cats	fish

   There are 2 more cats than fish.

15. Which one is $\frac{1}{2}$ full?

Score 15

Work it out!

TABLES

1. 10 + 2 = 12
2. 2 + 2 = 4
3. 8 + 2 = 10
4. 2 + 1 = 3
5. 8 + 2 = 10

6. I am a cube.

7. There are 7 days in a week.

8. It is 5 o'clock.

9. Tick the heavier one. ✓

10. $\frac{1}{2}$ of 20 is 10.

11. 2 + 2 + 2 + 2 = 8

12. A sphere has 0 corners.

13. Fill in the missing numbers.
    16, 17, 18, 19, 20, 21, 22 23

14. 2, 4, 6, 8, 10.
    I am counting in 2 s.

15. Barry
    is taller.

    Barry   Peter

Score 15

Page 66 for Friday Test – Week 2.

T A B L E S

1. $3 + 3 =$ ☐
2. $3 + 2 =$ ☐
3. $3 + 8 =$ ☐
4. $3 + 2 =$ ☐
5. $3 + 9 =$ ☐

6. Show 11 o'clock.

7. Colour half. ☐

8. How much? ☐ c

9. Today is _____.

10.

$=$ ☐ tens ☐ units

11. Ring the tens digit.   85

12. Double 20 = ☐

13.  A car is heavier ☐ lighter ☐ than 1 kg.

14. ☐ $- 2 = 5$

15. ☐ is $\frac{1}{2}$ of 4.

☹ ☐ 😐 ☐ ☺ ☐ Score ◯ 15

Work it out!

---

1. $3 + $ ☐ $= 5$
2. ☐ $+ 3 = 12$
3. ☐ $+ 3 = 10$
4. ☐ $+ 3 = 5$
5. ☐ $+ 3 = 4$
6. ☐ $+ 3 = 7$
7. ☐ $+ 3 = 9$
8. ☐ $+ 3 = 13$
9. ☐ $+ 3 = 6$
10. ☐ $+ 3 = 11$
11. $3 + $ ☐ $= 7$

12. $3 + $ ☐ $= 3$
13. $3 + $ ☐ $= 10$
14. $3 + $ ☐ $= 11$
15. ☐ $+ 3 = 8$
16. $3 + $ ☐ $= 9$
17. $3 + $ ☐ $= 12$
18. $3 + $ ☐ $= 6$
19. $3 + $ ☐ $= 8$
20. $3 + $ ☐ $= 13$

   Score 20

WEDNESDAY – WEEK 3

T A B L E S

1. $3 + \boxed{} = 9$
2. $3 + \boxed{} = 5$
3. $7 + 3 = \boxed{}$
4. $\boxed{} + 3 = 13$
5. $3 + 8 = \boxed{}$

6. A ball is the same shape as a sphere $\boxed{}$ a cube $\boxed{}$.

7. Tick the one that holds more water.  $\boxed{}$ $\boxed{}$

8. Ring the odd numbers. 2 3 4 5 6

9. Draw a line to show half.

10. How many do you need to buy a 40c bar? $\boxed{}$

11.

	5	
	4	
	3	
	2	
	1	
	ice-cream	chocolate

Which is the favourite? _____

12. $7 + \boxed{} = 12$

13. $43 - 3 = \boxed{}$

14. _____ is the 1st day of the week.

15. Yesterday was _____ .

 $\boxed{}$ $\boxed{}$ $\boxed{}$ Score $\boxed{\dfrac{}{15}}$

Work it out

THURSDAY – WEEK 3

T A B L E S

1. $3 + 4 = \boxed{}$
2. $3 + 8 = \boxed{}$
3. $3 + 9 = \boxed{}$
4. $3 + \boxed{} = 8$
5. $\boxed{} + 3 = 13$

6. Ring the tens digit. 39

7. Fill in the missing numbers.

36, 37, $\boxed{}$, 39, $\boxed{}$, $\boxed{}$

8. Colour $\frac{1}{2}$ of the 6 circles.

9. What time is it? It is _____ .

10. How much? $\boxed{}$ c

11. $= \boxed{}$ tens $\boxed{}$ unit

12. $22 - 10 = \boxed{}$

13. ⬭ I am a _____ .

14. Tick the longer one. $\boxed{}$ $\boxed{}$

15. Tick the heavier one. $\boxed{}$ $\boxed{}$

 $\boxed{}$ $\boxed{}$ $\boxed{}$ Score $\boxed{\dfrac{}{15}}$

T A B L E S

1. $4 + 10 = \boxed{}$
2. $4 + 8 = \boxed{}$
3. $4 + 7 = \boxed{}$
4. $4 + 9 = \boxed{}$
5. $4 + 6 = \boxed{}$

6. $(<, >, =)$ $2 + 1$ $\boxed{}$ 3

7. A cuboid has $\boxed{}$ faces.

8. $\frac{1}{2}$ of 10 is $\boxed{}$.

9. Draw beads to show 23.

T   U

10. $10 + 2 = 5 + \boxed{}$

11. Jim has 9 sweets. Alex has the same. They have $\boxed{}$ altogether.

12. April comes after _____.

13. There are $\boxed{}$ more bikes than scooters.

14. How many 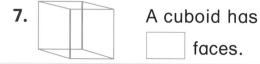 coins are needed to make 20c? $\boxed{}$

15. Shauna has 30 marbles. Seán has double that amount. How many marbles has Seán? $\boxed{}$

Score $\boxed{}$ $\boxed{}$ $\boxed{}$ / 15

Work it out

1. $4 + \boxed{} = 10$
2. $\boxed{} + 4 = 14$
3. $\boxed{} + 4 = 6$
4. $\boxed{} + 4 = 10$
5. $\boxed{} + 4 = 5$
6. $\boxed{} + 4 = 8$
7. $\boxed{} + 4 = 13$
8. $\boxed{} + 4 = 12$
9. $\boxed{} + 4 = 7$
10. $\boxed{} + 4 = 11$
11. $4 + \boxed{} = 12$

12. $4 + \boxed{} = 7$
13. $4 + \boxed{} = 9$
14. $4 + \boxed{} = 6$
15. $\boxed{} + 4 = 9$
16. $4 + \boxed{} = 5$
17. $4 + \boxed{} = 11$
18. $4 + \boxed{} = 8$
19. $4 + \boxed{} = 4$
20. $4 + \boxed{} = 13$

Score $\boxed{}$ $\boxed{}$ $\boxed{}$ / 20

10

WEDNESDAY – WEEK 4

TABLES

1. $4 + \boxed{} = 14$

2. $4 + \boxed{} = 10$

3. $5 + 4 = \boxed{}$

4. $\boxed{} + 4 = 4$

5. $4 + 6 = \boxed{}$

6. Ring the units digit.   29

7. Finish the pattern.

△ ▢ ⬭ △ __ __ __

8. I kg of sugar weighs the same as I kg of potatoes. Yes ▢ No ▢

9. Which number is the odd one out? 2, 4, 5, 8, 10 ▢

10. Ring the coins you need.

25c

11. $18 - \boxed{} = 11$

12. Ring the number with 3 in the units place.   35   43

13. Philip has 40 marbles. What is half his number? ▢

14. There are ▢ days in June.

15. Tick the one that holds more. ▢ ▢

☹▢ 😐▢ ☺▢ Score ⊘ 15

Work it out!

THURSDAY – WEEK 4

TABLES

1. $0 + 4 = \boxed{}$

2. $4 + 1 = \boxed{}$

3. $4 + 6 = \boxed{}$

4. $4 + \boxed{} = 6$

5. $\boxed{} + 4 = 8$

6. Colour half.

7. 2, 4, 6, 8. These are even ▢ odd ▢ numbers.

8. True or false: An eggcup holds more than I litre. _____

9. What is $\frac{1}{2}$ of 50? ▢

10.
6		
5		
4		
3		
2		
1		
	football	swimming

Which is more popular? _____

11. 🍎 12c 🍒 15c How much? ▢ c

12. Barry Paul Mark Peter   Paul is in ▢ place.

13. 20, 30, ▢, ▢, 60, ▢, 80

14. $30 - \boxed{} = 20$

15. What time is it? It is _____.

☹▢ 😐▢ ☺▢ Score ⊘ 15

☞ Page 67 for Friday Test – Week 4.

T A B L E S

1. $5 + 5 =$ ☐
2. $5 + 2 =$ ☐
3. $5 + 6 =$ ☐
4. $5 + 10 =$ ☐
5. $5 + 8 =$ ☐

6. Draw half a circle.

7. ⚫⚫⚫⚫⚫⚫⚫⚫⚫⚫ ⚫⚫⚫ = ☐

8. What is double 30? ☐

9. I have one square corner. How many square corners has a square? ☐

10.  What time is one hour later? ☐ o'clock

11. $6 + 3 + 2 =$ ☐

12. In what season is May?
It is in _____.

13. $(<, >, =)$ $4 + 2$ ☐ 5

14. What shape am I?
I am a _____.

15.  How much? ☐ c

☹ ☐   😐 ☐   🙂 ☐   Score ◯ 15

Work it out!

1. $5 + $ ☐ $ = 7$
2. ☐ $ + 5 = 10$
3. ☐ $ + 5 = 14$
4. ☐ $ + 5 = 6$
5. ☐ $ + 5 = 12$
6. ☐ $ + 5 = 13$
7. ☐ $ + 5 = 15$
8. ☐ $ + 5 = 11$
9. ☐ $ + 5 = 9$
10. ☐ $ + 5 = 8$
11. $5 + $ ☐ $ = 6$

12. $5 + $ ☐ $ = 9$
13. $5 + $ ☐ $ = 11$
14. $5 + $ ☐ $ = 5$
15. ☐ $ + 5 = 7$
16. $5 + $ ☐ $ = 8$
17. $5 + $ ☐ $ = 13$
18. $5 + $ ☐ $ = 15$
19. $5 + $ ☐ $ = 12$
20. $5 + $ ☐ $ = 10$

☹ ☐   😐 ☐   🙂 ☐   Score ◯ 20

WEDNESDAY – WEEK 5

TABLES

1. $5 + \boxed{} = 10$
2. $5 + \boxed{} = 9$
3. $2 + 5 = \boxed{}$
4. $\boxed{} + 5 = 8$
5. $5 + 8 = \boxed{}$

6. $\frac{1}{2}$ of 10 is $\boxed{}$.

7. Ring the lowest number.

   20   12   31

8. $4 + 9 + \boxed{} = 15$

9. How many days in a week? $\boxed{}$

10. Sue has 9 sweets. Jim has 8 more. How many has Jim? $\boxed{}$

11. 6 is an even ☐ odd ☐ number.

12. A ruler is lighter ☐ heavier ☐ than 1 kg.

13. Ring the tens digit.   50

14. Share 10 bananas between 2 monkeys. How many will they get each? $\boxed{}$

15. What shape am I?

    I am a _____.

☹ ☐ 😐 ☐ ☺ ☐ Score ⊘ 15

Work it out!

THURSDAY – WEEK 5

TABLES

1. $5 + 10 = \boxed{}$
2. $9 + 5 = \boxed{}$
3. $5 + 8 = \boxed{}$
4. $5 + \boxed{} = 14$
5. $\boxed{} + 5 = 7$

6. Colour half of the 12 circles. ○○○○○○ ○○○○○○

7. Write the number before 40. $\boxed{}$

8. Emma has 10 balls. Josh has 12. Josh has $\boxed{}$ more than Emma.

9. Fill in the missing number.

   5, 10, $\boxed{}$, 20

10. $(<, >, =)$ 9 $\boxed{}$ 7

11. There are $\boxed{}$ months in a season.

12. Tick the one that holds more.

13. $2 + 10 = \boxed{} + 8$

14. I need $\boxed{}$ 20c coins to buy a 40c drink.

15. What time is 1 hour after 3 o'clock? $\boxed{}$ o'clock

☹ ☐ 😐 ☐ ☺ ☐ Score ⊘ 15

TABLES

1. $6 + 2 =$ ☐
2. $6 + 10 =$ ☐
3. $6 + 8 =$ ☐
4. $6 + 2 =$ ☐
5. $6 + 3 =$ ☐

6. $\frac{1}{2}$ of 12 is ☐ .

7. A square has 4 square corners.
   A rectangle has ☐ .

8. 8 is ☐ less than 10.

9. Colour the oval.

10. $40 + 7 =$ ☐

11. Show half past 12.

12. There are 100 cm in 1 m.
    How many cm in $\frac{1}{2}$ m? ☐

13.  $=$ ☐

14.  How much? ☐ c

15. Fill in the missing number.
    2, 4, ☐ , 8, 10

☹ ☐ 😐 ☐ ☺ ☐ Score ⊘ 15

Work it out!

1. $6 + $ ☐ $= 9$
2. ☐ $+ 6 = 14$
3. ☐ $+ 6 = 11$
4. ☐ $+ 6 = 15$
5. ☐ $+ 6 = 12$
6. ☐ $+ 6 = 16$
7. ☐ $+ 6 = 10$
8. ☐ $+ 6 = 13$
9. ☐ $+ 6 = 7$
10. ☐ $+ 6 = 9$
11. $6 + $ ☐ $= 12$

12. $6 + $ ☐ $= 14$
13. $6 + $ ☐ $= 7$
14. $6 + $ ☐ $= 13$
15. ☐ $+ 6 = 8$
16. $6 + $ ☐ $= 8$
17. $6 + $ ☐ $= 16$
18. $6 + $ ☐ $= 10$
19. $6 + $ ☐ $= 15$
20. $6 + $ ☐ $= 11$

☹ ☐ 😐 ☐ ☺ ☐ Score ⊘ 20

14

WEDNESDAY – WEEK 6

T A B L E S

1. $6 + \boxed{} = 9$
2. $6 + \boxed{} = 7$
3. $6 + 6 = \boxed{}$
4. $\boxed{} + 6 = 6$
5. $7 + 6 = \boxed{}$

6. $\frac{1}{2}$ m $+ \frac{1}{2}$ m $= \boxed{}$ cm

7. Draw beads to show 40.

8. What time is it? It is
_____ .

9. $59 = \boxed{}$ tens and $\boxed{}$ units

10. Draw half an oval.

11. A cylinder has $\boxed{}$ flat faces.

12.  $= \boxed{}$

13. $50 + 5 = \boxed{}$

14. Name something that weighs less than 1 kg. _____

15. How many minutes in 1 hour?
$\boxed{}$

Score $\boxed{}$ / 15

Work it out!

THURSDAY – WEEK 6

T A B L E S

1. $0 + 6 = \boxed{}$
2. $1 + 6 = \boxed{}$
3. $6 + 8 = \boxed{}$
4. $6 + \boxed{} = 15$
5. $\boxed{} + 6 = 7$

6. There are $\boxed{}$ less pencils than rulers.

7. Colour the cone red.

8. $(<, >, =)$ $4 + 2$ $\boxed{}$ $2 + 4$

9. $10 + \boxed{} = 22$

10. Eva has 18 stickers. John has 10 more than Eva. John has $\boxed{}$.

11. What time is 1 hour after 3 o'clock? $\boxed{}$ o'clock

12. Tick the longer line.

13. How many 10c coins in €1? $\boxed{}$

14. $80 - 1 = \boxed{}$

15. Colour half of the 14 stars.

Score $\boxed{}$ / 15

T A B L E S

1. $7 + 7 =$ ☐
2. $7 + 3 =$ ☐
3. $7 + 9 =$ ☐
4. $7 + 2 =$ ☐
5. $7 + 6 =$ ☐

6. Estimate how many eggcups of water are needed to fill a jug. ☐

7. There are ☐ mins in a $\frac{1}{2}$ hour.

8. ◺ I have ☐ square corner.

9. 4 tens and 5 units = ☐

10. $\frac{1}{2}$ of 12 is ☐.

11. 63 units = ☐ tens + ☐ units.

12. 1 metre = ☐ cm

13.  = ☐

14. Start at 10. Jump back 3. I land on ☐.

15.  This is a _____.

☹ ☐ 😐 ☐ 🙂 ☐ Score ⊘ 15

Work it out!

1. $7 + $ ☐ $ = 15$
2. ☐ $ + 7 = 10$
3. ☐ $ + 7 = 16$
4. ☐ $ + 7 = 11$
5. ☐ $ + 7 = 14$
6. ☐ $ + 7 = 12$
7. ☐ $ + 7 = 17$
8. ☐ $ + 7 = 13$
9. ☐ $ + 7 = 7$
10. ☐ $ + 7 = 15$
11. $7 + $ ☐ $ = 11$

12. $7 + $ ☐ $ = 13$
13. $7 + $ ☐ $ = 8$
14. $7 + $ ☐ $ = 10$
15. ☐ $ + 7 = 9$
16. $7 + $ ☐ $ = 9$
17. $7 + $ ☐ $ = 16$
18. $7 + $ ☐ $ = 12$
19. $7 + $ ☐ $ = 7$
20. $7 + $ ☐ $ = 14$

☹ ☐ 😐 ☐ 🙂 ☐ Score ⊘ 20

TABLES

1. $7 + \boxed{} = 8$
2. $7 + \boxed{} = 15$
3. $9 + 7 = \boxed{}$
4. $\boxed{} + 7 = 13$
5. $7 + 4 = \boxed{}$

6. What time is it? It is _____.

7. $\frac{1}{2}$ of 14 is $\boxed{}$.

8. $= \boxed{}$

9. $20 + 20 = \boxed{}$

10. What number comes after 75? $\boxed{}$

11.  What shape am I?
    I am a _____.

12. Name something that weighs more than 1 kg. _____.

13. 3 tens and 7 units $= \boxed{}$

14. Is water measured in litres or metres? _____.

15. $74 = \boxed{}$ tens and $\boxed{}$ units

☹ ☐ ☺ ☐ ☺ ☐ Score ⊘ 15

Work it out!

TABLES

1. $7 + 4 = \boxed{}$
2. $7 + 5 = \boxed{}$
3. $2 + 7 = \boxed{}$
4. $7 + \boxed{} = 10$
5. $\boxed{} + 7 = 9$

6. $(<, >, =)$ $7 - 0 \boxed{} 9 - 1$

7. $= \boxed{}$

8. $\boxed{}$ is $\frac{1}{2}$ of 14.

9. Start at 18. Jump back 6.
    I land on $\boxed{}$.

10. Is height measured in litres or metres? _____.

11. 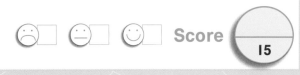 How much? $\boxed{}$ c

12. Colour the tallest girl.

13. Christmas is in _____.

14. Fill in the missing numbers.
    74, 75, 76, 77, 78, $\boxed{}$, $\boxed{}$, 81

15. $24 + 6 = \boxed{}$

☹ ☐ ☺ ☐ ☺ ☐ Score ⊘ 15

☞ Page 69 for Friday Test – Week 7.

T A B L E S

1. $8 + 10 = 18$
2. $8 + 3 = 11$
3. $8 + 2 = 10$
4. $8 + 6 = 14$
5. $8 + 9 = 17$

6. I am a flat shape with 3 sides.
   I am a _triangle_ .

7. True or false: There are 1000 ml in 1 litre. _true_

8. Share (colour) 20 sweets between 2 so that each gets $\frac{1}{2}$. _10_

9. I had 20 lollipops. I ate 4. I have [16] left.

10. What day will it be tomorrow? _Tuesday_

11. $\frac{1}{2}$ metre = [15] cm

12. $3 + 10 = 5 + [8]$

13. $27 = [2]$ tens $+ [7]$ units

14. [50c] 50c coins = €1.

15. ⟶ I have [ ] square corners.

☹ [ ] 😐 [ ] 🙂 [ ] **Score** ⊘ 15

Work it out!

---

1. $8 + [7] = 15$
2. $[3] + 8 = 11$
3. $[7] + 8 = 15$
4. $[4] + 8 = 12$
5. $[8] + 8 = 16$
6. $[5] + 8 = 13$
7. $[10] + 8 = 18$
8. $[0] + 8 = 8$
9. $[9] + 8 = 17$
10. $[2] + 8 = 10$
11. $8 + [2] = 10$

12. $8 + [5] = 13$
13. $8 + [9] = 17$
14. $8 + [3] = 11$
15. $[6] + 8 = 14$
16. $8 + [8] = 16$
17. $8 + [1] = 9$
18. $8 + [6] = 14$
19. $8 + [0] = 8$
20. $8 + [4] = 12$

☹ [ ] 😐 [ ] 🙂 [ ] **Score** ⊘ 20

TABLES

1. 8 + [5] = 13
2. 8 + [1] = 9
3. 8 + 0 = [8]
4. [2] + 8 = 10
5. 7 + 8 = [15]

6. Colour half.

7. 10 cows, 15 sheep and 14 pigs. How many animals? [39]

8. 58 = [5] tens + [8] units

9.  How much? [90]c
   (40c) (50c)

10. A farmer had 23 horses. She sold 5. How many are left? [17]

11. What time is it? It is half past 3.

12. 3 + 3 + 3 + 3 = [12]

13. Name something that weighs about 1 kg. flour

14. What month will it be next month? June

15. 20 less than 30 is [10].

☹ □ 😐 □ 🙂 □ Score [/15]

Work it out.

TABLES

1. 8 + 0 = [8]
2. 8 + 1 = [9]
3. 9 + 8 = [17]
4. 8 + [4] = 12
5. [7] + 8 = 15

6. True or false: Liquid is measured in litres. True

7. Tick the one that is about half full. □ □ ✓

8. A car carries 5 people. Two cars can carry [10] people.

9. 3 + 6 + 10 = [19]

10. Tick the lighter one.  □ ✓

11. 1 hour after 6 o'clock is [7] o'clock.

12. True or false: A circle has 1 square corner. false

13. Colour ¼ of 8. ⊘⊘⊘○○○○○

14. Colour 25 cent.

15. Estimate how many squares are needed to cover the rectangle. [2]

☹ □ 😐 □ 🙂 □ Score [/15]

MONDAY – WEEK 9

TABLES

1. $9 + 0 = 9$
2. $9 + 1 = 10$
3. $9 + 4 = 13$
4. $9 + 8 = 17$
5. $9 + 5 = 14$

6. Ring the odd one out.

7. Tick the lighter one.  ✓

8. Colour $\frac{1}{2}$ of the 6 balloons.

9. There are 31 days in March.

10. This window has 4 square corners.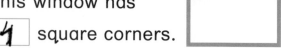

11. Tom has 10 pears. Alfie has 4 more. How many has Alfie? 14

12.  $= 35$

13. What three coins make 50 cent? 20 c, 20 c, 10 c

14. 4, 6, 8, 10, 12 is counting in 2 s.

15. $50 \text{ cm} + 50 \text{ cm} = 100$ metre

☹ ☺ 😊 Score 15

Work it out!

TABLES TUESDAY – WEEK 9

1. $9 + 4 = 14$
2. $3 + 9 = 11$
3. $7 + 9 = 16$
4. $0 + 9 = 9$
5. $4 + 9 = 13$
6. $5 + 9 = 14$
7. $8 + 9 = 17$
8. $10 + 9 = 19$
9. $6 + 9 = 15$
10. $9 + 9 = 18$
11. $9 + 10 = 19$

12. $9 + 1 = 10$
13. $9 + 8 = 17$
14. $9 + 3 = 11$
15. $4 + 9 = 12$
16. $9 + 7 = 16$
17. $9 + 3 = 12$
18. $9 + 6 = 15$
19. $9 + 9 = 18$
20. $9 + 4 = 13$

☹ ☺ 😊 Score 20

☞ Page 70 for Friday Test – Week 9.

TABLES

1. $9 + \boxed{} = 9$
2. $9 + \boxed{} = 16$
3. $9 + 4 = \boxed{}$
4. $\boxed{} + 9 = 13$
5. $9 + 9 = \boxed{}$

6. $\boxed{}$ This shape has square corners. True ☐ False ☐

7. 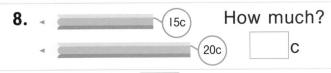 How many faces? $\boxed{}$

8. How much? $\boxed{}$ c
    15c
    20c

9. $40 + 20 = \boxed{}$

10. Tick the one that shows $\frac{1}{2}$.  ☐ ☐

11. True or false: Sugar is measured in millilitres. _____

12. $34 + 40 = \boxed{}$

13. 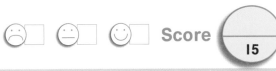 What time will it be in half an hour? _____

14. 5 more than 11 is $\boxed{}$.

15. Colour the 3rd star. ☆ ☆ ☆

☹ ☐ 😐 ☐ ☺ ☐ Score ⊘ 15

Work it out!

TABLES

1. $9 + 2 = \boxed{}$
2. $9 + 5 = \boxed{}$
3. $1 + 9 = \boxed{}$
4. $9 + \boxed{} = 12$
5. $\boxed{} + 9 = 13$

6. How many fingers have 3 children? $\boxed{}$

7. A swimming pool holds more ☐ less ☐ than 1 litre of water.

8. $(<, >, =)$ $4 + 5$ $\boxed{}$ $2 + 7$.

9. Fill in the missing numbers.
    10, 12, 14, $\boxed{}$, $\boxed{}$, 20, $\boxed{}$

10. $31 - 20 = \boxed{}$

11. $7 - \boxed{} = 5$

12.  Three stools have $\boxed{}$ legs.

13. How many days in 2 weeks? $\boxed{}$

14.  How long? (Use a ruler.) $\boxed{}$ cm

15. Colour half of the pizza. ◯

☹ ☐ 😐 ☐ ☺ ☐ Score ⊘ 15

TABLES

1. $10 + 3 = 13$
2. $10 + 4 = 14$
3. $10 + 5 = 15$
4. $10 + 6 = 16$
5. $10 + 7 = 17$

6. 5 tens and 7 units is greater ✓ less ☐ than 49.

7. A bucket holds more ✓ less ☐ than 1 litre of water.

8. I have 2 square corners. True ☐ False ✓

9. ☐ 20c coins = €1

10. Colour half of the 20 stars. 10

11. ☐ Is this shape symmetrical? Yes ✓ No ☐

12. How many squares are needed to cover the book? ☐

13. There are 30 mins in a ½ hour.

14. Tick the heavier one. 🕷 ☐ 📙 ✓

15. $10 + 12 = 20 + 4\ 2$

☹ ☐ 😐 ☐ ☺ ☐ Score 15

Work it out

1. $10 + 8 = 18$
2. $8 + 10 = 18$
3. $6 + 10 = 16$
4. $10 + 10 = 20$
5. $0 + 10 = 10$
6. $9 + 10 = 19$
7. $2 + 10 = 12$
8. $5 + 10 = 15$
9. $3 + 10 = 13$
10. $7 + 10 = 17$
11. $10 + 6 = 16$

12. $10 + 5 = 15$
13. $10 + 2 = 12$
14. $10 + 10 = 20$
15. $1 + 10 = 11$
16. $10 + 7 = 17$
17. $10 + 1 = 11$
18. $10 + 9 = 19$
19. $10 + 4 = 14$
20. $10 + 3 = 13$

☹ ☐ 😐 ☐ ☺ ☐ Score 20

TABLES

1. $10 + \boxed{} = 20$
2. $10 + \boxed{} = 16$
3. $10 + 3 = \boxed{}$
4. $\boxed{} + 10 = 18$
5. $5 + 10 = \boxed{}$

6. Is this shape symmetrical? Yes ☐ No ☐

7. A tricycle has 3 wheels. How many wheels on 2 tricycles? $\boxed{}$

8. △ I am a _____.

9. $\frac{1}{2}$ metre $+ \frac{1}{2}$ metre $= \boxed{}$ metre

10. $\boxed{} + 15 = 30$

11. $138 = \boxed{}$ hundred, $\boxed{}$ tens and $\boxed{}$ units

12. How many days are in 2 weeks? $\boxed{}$

13. Colour $\frac{1}{2}$ of the heart.

14. The jar holds 1 litre. How much water is in it? $\frac{1}{2}$ litre ☐ $\frac{1}{4}$ litre ☐

15. $50c + 20c + 20c + \boxed{} c = €1$

 Score ⊘ / 15

Work it out!

TABLES

1. $10 + 4 = \boxed{}$
2. $10 + 2 = \boxed{}$
3. $8 + 10 = \boxed{}$
4. $10 + \boxed{} = 15$
5. $\boxed{} + 10 = 16$

6. 3, 6, 9, 12 is counting in $\boxed{}$ s.

7. [32 sweets] [21 sweets] How many sweets? $\boxed{}$

8. $(<, >, =)$ $5 + 3 \boxed{} 10 - 2$

9. 9 tens and 1 unit $= \boxed{}$

10. Fill in the missing numbers.
    3, $\boxed{}$, 9, $\boxed{}$, $\boxed{}$

11. 10 fewer than 20 is $\boxed{}$.

12. How many faces? $\boxed{}$

13. Draw a line of symmetry on this square.

14. What must I add to 42 to make 45? $\boxed{}$

15. 1 kg of flour costs €1. How much does a $\frac{1}{2}$ kg cost? $\boxed{}$ c

 Score ⊘ / 15

MONDAY – WEEK 11

TABLES

1. 1 + 5 = ☐
2. 1 + 9 = ☐
3. 1 + 0 = ☐
4. 2 + 3 = ☐
5. 2 + 7 = ☐

6. How many petals? ☐

7. 🪙 🪙 🪙 🪙 = ☐ c

8. Tick the one that shows ½. ☐ ☐

9. I am a _____.

10. A spoon holds more ☐ less ☐ than 1 litre.

11. Write 8 o'clock on the digital clock. ⬜ :

12. 6 cats, 5 dogs, 3 fish, 1 hamster. How many pets? ☐

13. Is this shape symmetrical? Yes ☐ No ☐

14. What must I add to 61 to make 71? ☐

15. Jill has 30 flowers. Tim has 10 more. How many has Tim? ☐

☹ ☐ 😐 ☐ 😊 ☐ Score ⊘ 15

Work it out.

TABLES TUESDAY – WEEK 11

1. 1 + ☐ = 7
2. 1 + ☐ = 3
3. 2 + ☐ = 10
4. 2 + ☐ = 2
5. 1 + ☐ = 6
6. 1 + ☐ = 5
7. 1 + ☐ = 2
8. 2 + ☐ = 11
9. 2 + ☐ = 6
10. 1 + ☐ = 10
11. 1 + ☐ = 9

12. 1 + ☐ = 4
13. 2 + ☐ = 12
14. 2 + ☐ = 8
15. 2 + ☐ = 4
16. 1 + ☐ = 11
17. 2 + ☐ = 5
18. 2 + ☐ = 9
19. 2 + ☐ = 7
20. 1 + ☐ = 8

☹ ☐ 😐 ☐ 😊 ☐ Score ⊘ 20

TABLES

1. ☐ + 2 = 10
2. ☐ + 1 = 5
3. ☐ + 1 = 1
4. ☐ + 2 = 4
5. ☐ + 2 = 12

6.  How many crayons? ☐

7. (?c) + (€10) + (5c) = 35c ☐ c

8. Colour $\frac{1}{2}$.

9. How many months are there in half a year? ☐

10. 2 dogs have ☐ legs.

11. When I cut a circle in half I get two s_____-c_____.

12.  How many edges? ☐

13.  Is it symmetrical along the dotted line? Yes ☐ No ☐

14. 5 + 5 + 5 + 5 = ☐

15. The height of a door is more ☐ less ☐ than 1 metre.

☹ ☐ 😐 ☐ 🙂 ☐ Score ⊘ 15

Work it out!

TABLES

1. 2 + 3 = ☐
2. 2 + 4 = ☐
3. 1 + 6 = ☐
4. 2 + ☐ = 10
5. ☐ + 2 = 7

6. 65 = ☐ tens and ☐ units

7. How many petals? ☐

8. A bag of sand weighs 1 kg. How much do 2 bags weigh? ☐ kg

9. (25c) (25c) How much? ☐ c

10. (<, >, =) 10 − 3 ☐ 7 + 2

11. There are 35 sweets. Paul eats 10. How many are left? ☐

12. When I cut a square in half I get two _____.

13.  This pizza is cut in $\frac{1}{2}$ ☐ $\frac{1}{4}$s ☐.

14. What time is it? It is _____.

15. How much juice is in the jug? ☐ l

☹ ☐ 😐 ☐ 🙂 ☐ Score ⊘ 15

☞ Page 71 for Friday Test – Week 11.

MONDAY – WEEK 12

T A B L E S

1. 3 + 6 = ▢

2. 3 + 1 = ▢

3. 3 + 8 = ▢

4. 4 + 8 = ▢

5. 4 + 5 = ▢

6. (16 + 1) + 1 = ▢

7. 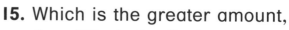 = ▢ c

8. How many days in 3 weeks? ▢

9. Colour $\frac{1}{4}$. ▢▢▢▢

10. Which digit has the greater value in the number 63? ▢

11. Is this a square corner? Yes ▢ No ▢

12. How many square corners inside this shape? ▢

13. How many faces? ▢

14. Is it symmetrical along the dotted line? Yes ▢ No ▢

15. Which is the greater amount, A or B? A  B  ▢

☹ ▢ 😐 ▢ ☺ ▢ Score ◯ 15

Work it out

TABLES TUESDAY – WEEK 12

1. 4 + ▢ = 8

2. 3 + ▢ = 7

3. 3 + ▢ = 9

4. 4 + ▢ = 12

5. 3 + ▢ = 5

6. 3 + ▢ = 13

7. 3 + ▢ = 8

8. 4 + ▢ = 4

9. 4 + ▢ = 13

10. 4 + ▢ = 10

11. 3 + ▢ = 12

12. 3 + ▢ = 6

13. 4 + ▢ = 11

14. 4 + ▢ = 7

15. 4 + ▢ = 6

16. 3 + ▢ = 11

17. 4 + ▢ = 14

18. 4 + ▢ = 9

19. 3 + ▢ = 10

20. 3 + ▢ = 4

☹ ▢ 😐 ▢ ☺ ▢ Score ◯ 20

☞ Page 71 for Friday Test – Week 12.
 Photocopying is prohibited

TABLES

1. ☐ + 4 = 12
2. ☐ + 3 = 6
3. ☐ + 3 = 10
4. ☐ + 3 = 4
5. ☐ + 3 = 13

6. Draw a line to divide the T-shirt in half.

7. 11 units = ☐ ten and ☐ unit

8. 5c + 5c + 5c + ☐ c = 20c

9. My maths book is more ☐ less ☐ than 1 metre wide.

10. (<, >, =) 10 ☐ 2 + 5 + 1

11. 2 hours before 11 o'clock is ☐ o'clock.

12. ☐ A square corner is also called a right angle. How many can you see? ☐

13. ¼ is coloured. Yes ☐ No ☐

14.  How much for 6 lollipops? ☐ c
    5c

15. Colour the jug to show 1 l.

☹ ☐ 😐 ☐ 🙂 ☐ Score ☐ / 15

Work it out.

TABLES

1. 4 + 8 = ☐
2. 3 + 9 = ☐
3. 3 + 4 = ☐
4. 3 + ☐ = 13
5. ☐ + 4 = 10

6. Colour ½ of the 4 apples.

7. Is a circle symmetrical?
   Yes ☐ No ☐

8. 5 is half of ☐.

9. What day comes after Thursday?
   _____ .

10. How many 1 kg bags of sugar to balance a 3 kg bag of flour? ☐

11. 40 + 5 = ☐

12. 7 + 0 = ☐

13. How much juice is in the jug? ☐ l

14. How many right angles inside this shape? ☐
    right angle

15. What time is it? It is _____ .

☹ ☐ 😐 ☐ 🙂 ☐ Score ☐ / 15

TABLES

1. $5 + 8 =$ ▢
2. $5 + 9 =$ ▢
3. $5 + 4 =$ ▢
4. $6 + 7 =$ ▢
5. $6 + 9 =$ ▢

6. Colour the jug to show $\frac{1}{4}$ l.

7. €1 – 50c = ▢ c

8. Estimate the length of your bed.
   ($\frac{1}{2}$ m, 1 m, 2 m, 3 m) ▢

9. Show $\frac{1}{4}$ past 6.

10. There are 20 children in a class. 8 are boys. How many girls? ▢

11. Draw a line of symmetry.

12. Oliver had 64 cards. He lost 15. How many has he left? ▢

13. Colour one-quarter.

14. Christmas Day is Dec ▢ th.

15. $36 +$ ▢ $= 48$

 Score 15

Work it out.

1. $5 +$ ▢ $= 11$
2. $5 +$ ▢ $= 13$
3. $6 +$ ▢ $= 10$
4. $5 +$ ▢ $= 6$
5. $5 +$ ▢ $= 7$
6. $6 +$ ▢ $= 6$
7. $6 +$ ▢ $= 9$
8. $5 +$ ▢ $= 8$
9. $6 +$ ▢ $= 12$
10. $5 +$ ▢ $= 15$
11. $6 +$ ▢ $= 11$

12. $5 +$ ▢ $= 14$
13. $5 +$ ▢ $= 10$
14. $6 +$ ▢ $= 15$
15. $6 +$ ▢ $= 14$
16. $6 +$ ▢ $= 8$
17. $6 +$ ▢ $= 16$
18. $6 +$ ▢ $= 13$
19. $5 +$ ▢ $= 9$
20. $5 +$ ▢ $= 12$

 Score 20

WEDNESDAY – WEEK 13

TABLES

1. ☐ + 5 = 15
2. ☐ + 6 = 16
3. ☐ + 6 = 8
4. ☐ + 6 = 10
5. ☐ + 6 = 11

6. Draw a line of symmetry.

7. Paul ate $\frac{1}{4}$ of the sweets. How many did he eat? ☐

8. The _____ holds more liquid. The _____ holds less.

jug

cup

9. ◯c + ◯c + ◯c = 70c

10. How many faces? ☐

11. There are 50 apples in a box. Half are bad. How many are good? ☐

12. 10 + 30 + 2 = ☐

13. (<, >, =) 10 – 4 ☐ 2 + 5

14. Kim's birthday is in the 9th month, which is _____.

15. Half an hour before 2 o'clock is _____.

☹ ☐ 😐 ☐ ☺ ☐ Score ⊘ 15

Work it out!

THURSDAY – WEEK 13

TABLES

1. 5 + 5 = ☐
2. 5 + 4 = ☐
3. 5 + 8 = ☐
4. 5 + ☐ = 7
5. ☐ + 6 = 14

6. How many 1 kg boxes of cereal balance 2 kg? ☐

7. Draw a line of symmetry.

8. A stool has 3 legs. How many legs have 5 stools? ☐

9. 21 + 5 + ☐ = 27

10. There are 10 sweets in a tube. How many are in 3 tubes? ☐

11. Name a winter month. _____

12. 40 – 20 = ☐

13. Colour one-quarter.

14. How much juice is in the jug? ☐ l

15. Half an hour after 4 o'clock is _____.

☹ ☐ 😐 ☐ ☺ ☐ Score ⊘ 15

T A B L E S

1. $7 + 10 =$ ☐
2. $7 + 2 =$ ☐
3. $7 + 4 =$ ☐
4. $8 + 9 =$ ☐
5. $8 + 10 =$ ☐

6. Complete this symmetrical shape.

7. True or false: The length of a sofa is $\frac{1}{2}$ m. _____

8. What fraction is coloured? ☐

9. ◯c + ◯c + ◯c = 70c

10. Write half past 9 on the digital clock. [:]

11. ☐ $\frac{1}{2}$ litres are needed to fill a 1 litre container.

12. $3 + 3 + 3 + 3 =$ ☐

13. $40 + 30 =$ ☐

14. How many faces? ☐

15. 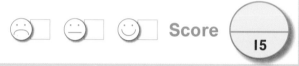 There are 10 sweets in each bag. How many sweets altogether? ☐

☹ ☐ ☺ ☐ ☺ ☐ Score ◯ 15

Work it out

1. $7 +$ ☐ $= 10$
2. $7 +$ ☐ $= 7$
3. $7 +$ ☐ $= 11$
4. $8 +$ ☐ $= 16$
5. $7 +$ ☐ $= 14$
6. $8 +$ ☐ $= 18$
7. $7 +$ ☐ $= 9$
8. $7 +$ ☐ $= 17$
9. $8 +$ ☐ $= 11$
10. $8 +$ ☐ $= 10$
11. $8 +$ ☐ $= 12$

12. $7 +$ ☐ $= 13$
13. $7 +$ ☐ $= 16$
14. $8 +$ ☐ $= 9$
15. $8 +$ ☐ $= 15$
16. $8 +$ ☐ $= 8$
17. $8 +$ ☐ $= 14$
18. $7 +$ ☐ $= 12$
19. $7 +$ ☐ $= 15$
20. $8 +$ ☐ $= 13$

☹ ☐ ☺ ☐ ☺ ☐ Score ◯ 20

☞ Page 72 for Friday Test – Week 14.  Photocopying is prohibited

TABLES

1. ☐ + 7 = 9
2. ☐ + 7 = 13
3. ☐ + 8 = 18
4. ☐ + 7 = 7
5. ☐ + 8 = 9

6. Complete this symmetrical shape.

7. Grace had 23 cards. She buys 10 more. How many has she? ☐

8. There are 10 sweets in a bag. How many are in 9 bags? ☐

9. 31 + 20 = 10 + 10 + 10 + 10 + 10 + ☐

10. What fraction is missing? ☐

11. Colour $\frac{1}{4}$ of the 12 fish.
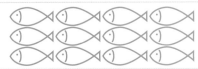

12. The big hand on the clock points to ☐ to show a quarter past.

13. 67, 68, ☐, ☐, ☐

14. 10 – 5 = 4 + ☐

15.  How much? € ☐

☹☐ ☺☐ ☺☐ Score ◯ 15

Work it out!

TABLES

1. 8 + 8 = ☐
2. 8 + 3 = ☐
3. 8 + 2 = ☐
4. 8 + ☐ = 18
5. ☐ + 8 = 12

6. There are 72 people on a train: 30 men, 21 women, ☐ children.

7. Half an hour before 9 o'clock is _____.

8. Fill in the missing numbers.
   5, 10, ☐, ☐, 25, ☐

9. (9 + 8) + 3 = ☐

10. Which season comes after spring? _____

11. Two $\frac{1}{2}$ litres will fill a ☐ litre container.

12. Tick the cylinder. ◯☐ ☐

13. Pat buys two 50c ice-creams. What change has he from €2? ☐

14. ☐ is 20 greater than 52.

15. A circle is ☐ is not ☐ symmetrical.

☹☐ ☺☐ ☺☐ Score ◯ 15

T A B L E S

1. $9 + 10 = \boxed{}$

2. $9 + 7 = \boxed{}$

3. $9 + 6 = \boxed{}$

4. $10 + 8 = \boxed{}$

5. $10 + 7 = \boxed{}$

6. Complete this symmetrical shape.

7. $(<, >, =)$ $3+3+3$ $\boxed{}$ $6+3$

8. $\boxed{}$ 20c coins make €1.

9. 10 is 5 less than $\boxed{}$.

10. There are $\boxed{}$ cm in $\frac{1}{2}$ metre.

11. $10 + 10 + 10 = 30$
$10 + 10 + 10 + 10 = \boxed{}$

12. $10 + \boxed{} + 5 = 32$

13.  What fraction is missing? $\boxed{}$

14. $\boxed{}$ $\frac{1}{4}$ litres will fill a 1 litre container.

15. New Year's Day is January $\boxed{}$ st.

☹ $\boxed{}$ 😐 $\boxed{}$ ☺ $\boxed{}$ Score $\frac{}{15}$

Work it out!

1. $9 + \boxed{} = 13$

2. $9 + \boxed{} = 17$

3. $10 + \boxed{} = 20$

4. $10 + \boxed{} = 12$

5. $9 + \boxed{} = 9$

6. $9 + \boxed{} = 12$

7. $10 + \boxed{} = 11$

8. $10 + \boxed{} = 19$

9. $9 + \boxed{} = 18$

10. $9 + \boxed{} = 19$

11. $10 + \boxed{} = 16$

12. $10 + \boxed{} = 18$

13. $10 + \boxed{} = 15$

14. $9 + \boxed{} = 16$

15. $9 + \boxed{} = 11$

16. $10 + \boxed{} = 17$

17. $10 + \boxed{} = 14$

18. $10 + \boxed{} = 13$

19. $9 + \boxed{} = 15$

20. $9 + \boxed{} = 14$

☹ $\boxed{}$ 😐 $\boxed{}$ ☺ $\boxed{}$ Score $\frac{}{20}$

☞ Page 73 for Friday Test – Week 15.

TABLES

1. ☐ + 10 = 18
2. ☐ + 10 = 19
3. ☐ + 9 = 11
4. ☐ + 9 = 14
5. ☐ + 10 = 13

6. Make €2 using 6 coins.

○ ○ ○ ○ ○ ○

7. How many spots? ☐

8. **04:30** What time is it? It is _____ .

9. 10 + 10 + 10 + 10 + 10 = ☐

10. How many ½ kg blocks of butter balance a 1 kg block? ☐

11. Half of 8 eggs in a box are broken. How many is that? ☐

12. Is 15 > 12? Yes ☐ No ☐

13. 10 tens make ☐ .

14. Colour the cube.

15. How much? € ☐

☹ ☐ 😐 ☐ ☺ ☐ Score ⊘ 15

Work it out!

TABLES

1. 9 + 4 = ☐
2. 10 + 4 = ☐
3. 10 + 10 = ☐
4. 10 + ☐ = 15
5. ☐ + 9 = 14

6. 10 – 2 – 5 – 2 = ☐ c

7. There are 10 sweets in a bag. How many sweets in 3 bags? ☐

8. Write 12 o'clock on the digital clock. [:]

9. Is 2 + 2 = 4 + 1? Yes ☐ No ☐

10. ☐ How many lines of symmetry has a square? ☐

11. A ♡ is ☐ is not ☐ a symmetrical shape.

12. ☐ ½ litres will fill a 2 litre container.

13. (½, ¼) 10c is ☐ of 20c.

14. 10 + ☐ + 8 = 40

15. Show a quarter to 4.

☹ ☐ 😐 ☐ ☺ ☐ Score ⊘ 15

☞ Page 73 for Friday Test – Week 15.

TABLES

1. 6 – 1 = 5
2. 10 – 1 = 9
3. 8 – 1 = 7
4. 12 – 2 = 10
5. 9 – 2 = 7

6. 10 10 10 10 10 10 10 10 10 10 = 100 sweets

7. How many $\frac{1}{2}$ m are needed to make 1 m? 2

8. 5 cm is $\frac{1}{2}$ of 10 cm.

9. Fill in the missing numbers.
4, 8, 12, 16, 20, 24, 28

10. 50c – 20c = 30 c

11.  Which is the more popular fruit? apples

12. 14 + 10 + 6 = 30

13. A die is the same shape as a cube.

14. [ ] $\frac{1}{4}$ litres will fill a $\frac{1}{2}$ litre container.

15. What time is it? It is quarter to 7.

☹ ☺ Score 15

Work it out!

---

1. 4 – 2 = 2
2. 5 – 1 = 4
3. 8 – 1 = 7
4. 6 – 1 = 5
5. 10 – 1 = 9
6. 9 – 1 = 8
7. 3 – 1 = 2
8. 7 – 1 = 6
9. 4 – 1 = 3
10. 1 – 1 = 0
11. 12 – 2 = 10

12. 7 – 2 = 5
13. 9 – 2 = 7
14. 2 – 2 = 0
15. 11 – 1 = 10
16. 5 – 2 = 3
17. 11 – 2 = 9
18. 6 – 2 = 4
19. 8 – 2 = 6
20. 10 – 2 = 8

☹ ☺ Score 20

WEDNESDAY – WEEK 16

TABLES

1. $4 - 1 = 3$
2. $2 - 1 = 1$
3. $7 - 2 = 5$
4. $7 - 1 = 6$
5. $5 - 1 = 4$

6. 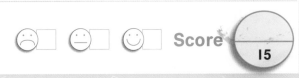 How much? 1.80 c

7. Paul has 20c. He spends $\frac{1}{4}$. How much has he left? ☐ c

8. There are 25 cm in $\frac{1}{4}$ m. How many cm in $\frac{1}{2}$ m? ☐

9. $70 - 5 = 65$

10. Tick the shape that can roll.  ✓

11. Tom has 9 DVDs. Sam has the same. Together they have 18.

12. Complete this symmetrical shape.

13. 10 cm is $\frac{1}{4}$ of ☐ cm.

14. 98, 99, ☐, ☐, ☐

15. **09:00** Show this time on the clock.

☹ ☐ ☺ ☐ 😊 ☐ Score ☐ / 15

Work it out

THURSDAY – WEEK 16

TABLES

1. $12 - 2 =$ ☐
2. $9 - 1 =$ ☐
3. $10 - 1 =$ ☐
4. $6 - 2 =$ ☐
5. $8 - 1 =$ ☐

6. $4 + 4 + 4 =$ ☐

7. What is the total weight of 2 $\frac{1}{2}$ kg boxes of sweets? ☐ kg

8. There are ☐ months in $\frac{1}{2}$ a year.

9. Erin had 20 books. She bought 12 more and sold 8. How many has she left? ☐

10. A yoghurt pot holds $\frac{1}{4}$ l. How many are needed to fill a 1 l jug? ☐

11. How many vertices? ☐

12. **M** Is the letter M symmetrical? Yes ☐ No ☐

13. 98, ☐, ☐, 101, ☐

14. $20 + 40 +$ ☐ $= 70$

15. Draw the other $\frac{1}{2}$.

☹ ☐ ☺ ☐ 😊 ☐ Score ☐ / 15

TABLES

1. $13 - 3 =$ ☐
2. $10 - 3 =$ ☐
3. $12 - 3 =$ ☐
4. $11 - 4 =$ ☐
5. $13 - 4 =$ ☐

6. 6c is $\frac{1}{2}$ of ☐ c.

7. Put $\frac{1}{2}$ l, 1 l and $\frac{1}{4}$ l in order starting with the smallest.

☐ l, ☐ l and ☐ l

8. What is 8 more than 10? ☐

9. Fill in the missing numbers.

98, 99, 100, ☐, ☐

10. I have 50c. How much change will I get if I spend 38c? ☐ c

11. $6 + 2 +$ ☐ $= 10$

12. A b_____ is a symmetrical insect that can fly.

13.  How much? € ☐

14. ($<$, $>$, $=$) $15 - 5$ ☐ $12 - 3$

15. Write this time on the digital clock. ☐ : ☐

☹ ☐ 😐 ☐ ☺ ☐ Score ⬭ 15

Work it out!

1. $6 - 4 =$ ☐
2. $11 - 3 =$ ☐
3. $12 - 3 =$ ☐
4. $8 - 3 =$ ☐
5. $6 - 3 =$ ☐
6. $13 - 3 =$ ☐
7. $10 - 3 =$ ☐
8. $3 - 3 =$ ☐
9. $9 - 3 =$ ☐
10. $5 - 3 =$ ☐
11. $14 - 4 =$ ☐

12. $8 - 4 =$ ☐
13. $10 - 4 =$ ☐
14. $12 - 4 =$ ☐
15. $7 - 3 =$ ☐
16. $13 - 4 =$ ☐
17. $9 - 4 =$ ☐
18. $11 - 4 =$ ☐
19. $4 - 4 =$ ☐
20. $7 - 4 =$ ☐

☹ ☐ 😐 ☐ ☺ ☐ Score ⬭ 20

Page 74 for Friday Test – Week 17.

WEDNESDAY – WEEK 17

T A B L E S

1. 10 − 3 = ☐
2. 12 − 3 = ☐
3. 8 − 3 = ☐
4. 6 − 3 = ☐
5. 4 − 3 = ☐

6. Harry has 3 sweets. Jenny has 10 bags with 10 sweets in each bag. Together they have ☐ sweets.

7. 4 + 4 + ☐ = 12

8. $\frac{1}{4}$ m = ☐ cm

9. If last month was February, next month will be _____.

10. (<, >, =) 2 + 4 ☐ 4 + 1

11. A _____ is a 3D shape that only has one face.

12. How much juice is in the jug? ☐ l

13. Tick which is $\frac{1}{2}$ of 16. 6 ☐ 8 ☐

14. Fill in the missing numbers.
107, 108, 109, ☐ , ☐

15. Show a quarter past 6.

😞 ☐ 😐 ☐ 🙂 ☐ Score ⊘ 15

Work it out!

THURSDAY – WEEK 17

T A B L E S

1. 4 − 4 = ☐
2. 11 − 4 = ☐
3. 12 − 4 = ☐
4. 10 − 4 = ☐
5. 9 − 4 = ☐

6. How much change will I get from €2 if I buy a ball for €1·50? ☐ c
   €1·50

7. 4, 8, ☐ , ☐ , ☐ , 24, 28,

8. ($\frac{1}{2}$, $\frac{1}{4}$, 1) 50 cm = ☐ m

9. Draw a line of symmetry.

10. ☐ months have 31 days.

11. How long? (Use a ruler.) ☐ cm

12. If half of 14 sweets are eaten, how many are left? ☐

13. A 3D shape that can be rolled but not stacked: _____

14. 4 is $\frac{1}{2}$ of ☐ .

15. May has 10 less books than Jen, who has 18. May has ☐ books.

😞 ☐ 😐 ☐ 🙂 ☐ Score ⊘ 15

MONDAY – WEEK 18

TABLES

1. 10 – 5 = **5**
2. 9 – 5 = **4**
3. 15 – 5 = **10**
4. 9 – 6 = **3**
5. 11 – 6 = **5**

6.  How much? € **1.53**

7. How long? (Use a ruler.) [ ] cm

_____

8. [grid image] $\frac{1}{2}$ of this chocolate bar has **4** squares.

9. (12 + 6 + 4) = (10 + **12**) = 22

10. Colour to show 1 $\frac{1}{2}$ l.

11. **O** Is the letter O symmetrical? Yes ✓ No ☐

12. **189** , **190** , 191, 192, 193

13. There are **24** months in 2 years.

14. Write half past 12 on the digital clock. **12 :30**

15. I can roll and slide but I cannot be stacked. I am a _____ .

☹ ☐ 😐 ☐ ☺ ☐ Score ◯ **15**

Work it out!

TABLES TUESDAY – WEEK 18

1. 8 – 6 = **2**
2. 11 – 5 = [ ]
3. 14 – 5 = [ ]
4. 5 – 5 = [ ]
5. 15 – 5 = [ ]
6. 12 – 5 = [ ]
7. 7 – 5 = [ ]
8. 9 – 5 = [ ]
9. 13 – 5 = [ ]
10. 8 – 5 = [ ]
11. 16 – 6 = [ ]

12. 6 – 6 = [ ]
13. 13 – 6 = [ ]
14. 11 – 6 = [ ]
15. 10 – 5 = [ ]
16. 14 – 6 = [ ]
17. 9 – 6 = [ ]
18. 15 – 6 = [ ]
19. 10 – 6 = [ ]
20. 12 – 6 = [ ]

   Score ◯ **20**

WEDNESDAY – WEEK 18

TABLES

1. 9 – 5 = ☐
2. 12 – 6 = ☐
3. 14 – 6 = ☐
4. 14 – 5 = ☐
5. 12 – 5 = ☐

6. (<, >, =) 24 ☐ 42

7. 10c + 20c + 5c + 2c = ☐ c

8. How many $\frac{1}{4}$ m make $\frac{1}{2}$ m? ☐

9. 163c = €☐

10. How many millilitres in 1 litre?
☐

11.  €1·55 How much change will I get from €2 if I buy a toy bus for €1·55? ☐ c

12. 7 is $\frac{1}{2}$ of ☐.

13. What time is it? It is _____.

14. $\frac{1}{4}$ of this chocolate bar has ☐ squares.

15. 90 + ☐ = 100

Score ☐ / 15

Work it out

THURSDAY – WEEK 18

TABLES

1. 12 – 6 = ☐
2. 5 – 5 = ☐
3. 7 – 5 = ☐
4. 9 – 6 = ☐
5. 16 – 6 = ☐

6.  + + ◯ = €1·60

7. Colour the shape that has 1 line of symmetry. ☐

8. How many $\frac{1}{4}$ m make 1 m? ☐

9. The 5th month of the year is _____.

10. 80 + 5 = ☐

11. February usually has ☐ days.

12. How many faces? ☐

13. $\frac{2}{4}$ of this chocolate bar have ☐ squares.

14. 9 is $\frac{1}{2}$ of ☐.

15. There are 10 cows, 7 sheep and 12 horses on a farm. How many animals are there altogether? ☐

Score ☐ / 15

MONDAY – WEEK 19

TABLES

1. $14 - 7 =$ ☐
2. $13 - 7 =$ ☐
3. $17 - 7 =$ ☐
4. $12 - 8 =$ ☐
5. $15 - 8 =$ ☐

6. What change will I get from €2 if I buy three 25c bars? € ☐

7. $20 + 30 + 40 =$ ☐

8. ☐ is $\frac{1}{4}$ of 8.

9. $10 +$ ☐ $= 40 + 5$

10. $125 =$ ☐ hundred, ☐ tens and ☐ units

11. Colour the shape with three faces.

12. June is the ☐ th month of the year.

13. Colour the shape with more than 1 line of symmetry.

14. $30 -$ ☐ $= 10$

15. Show this time on the clock.

☹ ☐ ☺ ☐ ☺ ☐ Score ⊕ 15

Work it out!

TABLES TUESDAY – WEEK 19

1. $13 - 8 =$ ☐
2. $10 - 7 =$ ☐
3. $16 - 7 =$ ☐
4. $11 - 7 =$ ☐
5. $17 - 7 =$ ☐
6. $8 - 7 =$ ☐
7. $13 - 7 =$ ☐
8. $14 - 7 =$ ☐
9. $9 - 7 =$ ☐
10. $12 - 7 =$ ☐
11. $16 - 8 =$ ☐

12. $8 - 8 =$ ☐
13. $17 - 8 =$ ☐
14. $11 - 8 =$ ☐
15. $15 - 7 =$ ☐
16. $12 - 8 =$ ☐
17. $14 - 8 =$ ☐
18. $10 - 8 =$ ☐
19. $18 - 8 =$ ☐
20. $15 - 8 =$ ☐

☹   ☺   ☺   Score 20

T A B L E S

1. 10 – 7 = ☐
2. 11 – 8 = ☐
3. 12 – 8 = ☐
4. 13 – 8 = ☐
5. 11 – 7 = ☐

6. How many $\frac{1}{2}$ kg packets of biscuits will balance 2 kg? ☐

7. How many cm in $\frac{1}{4}$ m? ☐

8. How long? (Use a ruler.) ☐ cm

9. Colour one-quarter.

10. (<, >, =) 20 – 5 ☐ 17 – 2

11. ☐ $\frac{1}{2}$ litres are needed to fill a 1 litre container.

12. Show a quarter to 4.

13. 20 is half of ☐.

14. 60 – 20 = ☐

15. Harry bought a 75c pack of stickers. How much change did he get from €2? € ☐

☹ ☐ 😐 ☐ 🙂 ☐ Score ☐ 15

Work it out!

T A B L E S

1. 18 – 8 = ☐
2. 14 – 7 = ☐
3. 16 – 7 = ☐
4. 11 – 8 = ☐
5. 10 – 8 = ☐

6. 60 = 10 + ☐ + ☐ + ☐ + ☐ + ☐

7. ☐ is $\frac{1}{4}$ of 8.

8. Is 24 > 42? Yes ☐ No ☐

9. Two rulers are 17 cm and 20 cm long. What is the difference in length between them? ☐ cm

10. There are ☐ minutes in one-quarter of an hour.

11. 24 + 30 = ☐

12. Complete this symmetrical shape.

13. 1 hundred, 2 tens, 5 units = ☐

14. Colour one-quarter. ☐☐☐☐

15. There are 8 apples in a box. $\frac{1}{4}$ are bad. ☐ are good.

☹ ☐ 😐 ☐ 🙂 ☐ Score ☐ 15

☞ Page 75 for Friday Test – Week 19.

MONDAY – WEEK 20

TABLES

1. $18 - 9 =$ ☐
2. $12 - 9 =$ ☐
3. $17 - 9 =$ ☐
4. $15 - 10 =$ ☐
5. $18 - 10 =$ ☐

6. Claire is 20 cm taller than Bart. Bart is 50 cm. Claire is ☐ cm.

7. Starting at zero I jump in 2s five times. Where do I land? ☐

8.  There are 6 eggs in a box. How many eggs in 7 boxes? ☐

9. $3 + 10 =$ ☐ $+ 0$

10. Emma has 50c. Paul has 20c more. How much has Paul? ☐ c

11. ☐ is the number before 57.

12. 2 is $\frac{1}{4}$ of ☐.

13. Complete this symmetrical shape.

14. 8 is $\frac{1}{2}$ of ☐.

15. Write this time on the digital clock. ☐ : ☐

☹ ☐ 😐 ☐ ☺ ☐ Score ☐ / 15

Work it out.

TABLES TUESDAY – WEEK 20

1. $19 - 10 =$ ☐
2. $12 - 9 =$ ☐
3. $19 - 9 =$ ☐
4. $15 - 9 =$ ☐
5. $9 - 9 =$ ☐
6. $18 - 9 =$ ☐
7. $17 - 9 =$ ☐
8. $13 - 9 =$ ☐
9. $16 - 9 =$ ☐
10. $11 - 9 =$ ☐
11. $17 - 10 =$ ☐

12. $10 - 10 =$ ☐
13. $20 - 10 =$ ☐
14. $13 - 10 =$ ☐
15. $14 - 9 =$ ☐
16. $16 - 10 =$ ☐
17. $18 - 10 =$ ☐
18. $12 - 10 =$ ☐
19. $15 - 10 =$ ☐
20. $14 - 10 =$ ☐

☹ ☐ 😐 ☐ ☺ ☐ Score ☐ / 20

WEDNESDAY – WEEK 20

T A B L E S

1. 20 – 10 = ☐
2. 19 – 10 = ☐
3. 16 – 10 = ☐
4. 17 – 9 = ☐
5. 12 – 9 = ☐

6. ⬭ I am symmetrical. True ☐ False ☐

7. ☐ , ☐ , 101, 102, 103

8. There are 17 girls and 15 boys in a class. How many children altogether? ☐

9. €1·52 = ☐ c

10. If 2 is $\frac{1}{4}$ of 8, what is $\frac{2}{4}$ of 8? ☐

11. I can slide and be stacked but I cannot roll. I am a r_____.

12. ☐ $\frac{1}{2}$ litres = 1 $\frac{1}{2}$ litres

13. Colour $\frac{2}{4}$. ☐☐☐☐

14.  Write this time on the digital clock. ☐ : ☐

15. Laura has three 20c coins. Paul has four 10c coins. Altogether they have € ☐ .

☹ ☐ 😐 ☐ ☺ ☐ Score ⊘ 15

Work it out ✏

THURSDAY – WEEK 20

T A B L E S

1. 16 – 9 = ☐
2. 17 – 10 = ☐
3. 18 – 9 = ☐
4. 16 – 10 = ☐
5. 15 – 10 = ☐

6. My birthday is in _____. It is in the ☐ month.

7. 153 = ☐ hundred, ☐ tens and ☐ units

8. If a 12 cm long worm grew 8 cm, how long would it be? ☐ cm

9. There are ☐ minutes in an hour.

10. If $\frac{1}{4}$ litre of ice-cream costs 40c, how much is $\frac{1}{2}$ litre? ☐ c

11. ☐ , 199, 198, 197, ☐

12. (16 + 12) – 11 = ☐

13. 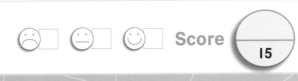 A cuboid's face is a r_____.

14. €2 How much more money does Leon need to buy the crayons if he has €1·24. ☐ c

15. $\frac{2}{4}$ of 12 is ☐ .

☹ ☐ 😐 ☐ ☺ ☐ Score ⊘ 15

 ☞ Page 75 for Friday Test – Week 20.

TABLES

1. 1 + 8 = ☐
2. 3 + 1 = ☐
3. 3 – 1 = ☐
4. 1 + 5 = ☐
5. 2 – 1 = ☐

6. Two 30 cm rulers = ☐ cm

7. €1 = 20c + ☐ c + ☐ c + ☐ c + ☐ c

8. 9 less than 20 is ☐.

9.  A fish weighs $\frac{1}{2}$ kg. What do 4 fish weigh? ☐ kg

10. 30 + 40 + ☐ = 80

11. A circle face can be found on a ☐☐ △☐.

12. Paul jumped $\frac{1}{2}$ m further than Áine. Áine jumped 70 cm. Paul jumped ☐ m ☐ cm.

13. 25 + 2 + ☐ = 30

14. Fill in the missing number.
156, 157, 158, 159, ☐

15. Write this time on the digital clock. ☐ : ☐

☹ ☐ 😐 ☐ ☺ ☐ Score ☐ / 15

Work it out

1. 7 – 1 = ☐
2. 7 + 1 = ☐
3. 4 – 1 = ☐
4. 10 – 1 = ☐
5. 1 + 4 = ☐
6. 1 + 8 = ☐
7. 3 – 1 = ☐
8. 9 – 1 = ☐
9. 5 + 1 = ☐
10. 3 + 1 = ☐
11. 11 – 1 = ☐

12. 8 – 1 = ☐
13. 1 + 0 = ☐
14. 1 + 2 = ☐
15. 1 + 9 = ☐
16. 6 – 1 = ☐
17. 10 + 1 = ☐
18. 1 + 6 = ☐
19. 5 – 1 = ☐
20. 1 – 1 = ☐

☹ ☐ 😐 ☐ ☺ ☐ Score ☐ / 20

TABLES

1. 1 + 7 = ☐
2. 1 + 8 = ☐
3. 8 – 1 = ☐
4. 1 + 3 = ☐
5. 6 – 1 = ☐

6. Is 52 < 25? Yes ☐ No ☐

7. ($\frac{1}{2}$ of 6) + ($\frac{1}{4}$ of 8) = ☐

8. Ahmed is 100 cm tall. Eimear is 85 cm tall. Together they are ☐ cm.

9. A bottle holds 1 litre. How many litres do 6 bottles hold? ☐ l

10. 40 + 35 = ☐

11. Draw the mirror image.

12. Half of 24 = ☐

13. 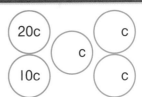 What time is it? It is _____.

14. 100 = 50 + 20 + ☐

15. Matt has 70c. Jake has €1·20. How much more money than Matt does Jake have? ☐ c

☹ ☐ 😐 ☐ 🙂 ☐ Score ☐ / 15

Work it out!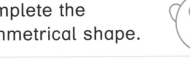

TABLES

1. 6 + 1 = ☐
2. 2 – 1 = ☐
3. 5 + 1 = ☐
4. 1 + 2 = ☐
5. 1 + 9 = ☐

6. 4 + 6 + 2 = 5 + ☐

7. What date is St Patrick's Day? _____.

8. ☐ is $\frac{1}{4}$ of 12 ★★★★★★ ★★★★★★

9. Complete the symmetrical shape.

10. 24 – 9 = ☐

11. What coins are needed to make €1?
    20c c c 10c c

12. ☐ c is 10c more than 20c.

13. ☐ hundred, ☐ tens and ☐ units = 156

14. A bottle of juice holds $\frac{1}{2}$ l. How many bottles are needed to fill a 2 l jug? ☐

15. 20 + 4 + ☐ = 30

☹ ☐ 😐 ☐ 🙂 ☐ Score ☐ / 15

☞ Page 76 for Friday Test – Week 21.

MONDAY – WEEK 22

TABLES

1. $2 + 8 =$ ▢

2. $10 + 2 =$ ▢

3. $5 - 2 =$ ▢

4. $3 + 2 =$ ▢

5. $2 - 2 =$ ▢

6. $48 =$ ▢ tens and ▢ units

7. $\frac{1}{2}$ of 12 is 6. What is $\frac{1}{4}$ of 12? ▢

8. What time is it? It is _____ .

9. $\frac{1}{4}$ m = ▢ cm

10. The width of my finger ▢ hand ▢ is used to measure 1 cm.

11. Write €1·62 in cent. ▢ c

12. Pauline spent $\frac{1}{2}$ her money on a pencil. How much did the pencil cost if she had €1·20? ▢ c

13. Ring the shape with two lines of symmetry.

14. I am a 3D shape with 3 faces. I am a _____ .

15. True or false: An aeroplane is symmetrical. _____

 Score ▢ / 15

Work it out!

TABLES TUESDAY – WEEK 22

1. $3 - 2 =$ ▢
2. $5 + 2 =$ ▢
3. $8 - 2 =$ ▢
4. $6 - 2 =$ ▢
5. $2 + 7 =$ ▢
6. $1 + 2 =$ ▢
7. $9 - 2 =$ ▢
8. $7 - 2 =$ ▢
9. $2 + 2 =$ ▢
10. $2 + 6 =$ ▢
11. $10 - 2 =$ ▢

12. $4 - 2 =$ ▢
13. $2 + 4 =$ ▢
14. $9 + 2 =$ ▢
15. $8 + 2 =$ ▢
16. $5 - 2 =$ ▢
17. $2 + 10 =$ ▢
18. $3 + 2 =$ ▢
19. $12 - 2 =$ ▢
20. $11 - 2 =$ ▢

   Score 20

46
Page 76 for Friday Test – Week 22.

WEDNESDAY – WEEK 22

T A B L E S

1. 2 + 5 = ☐
2. 9 + 2 = ☐
3. 4 – 2 = ☐
4. 8 + 2 = ☐
5. 10 – 2 = ☐

6. Write the number before 180. ☐

7. How many $\frac{1}{2}$ kg bags of sugar are needed to balance 3 kg? ☐

8. (12 + 4) + 5 = ☐

9. Estimate how many centimetres long your pencil is using the width of your finger. ☐ cm

10. 03:30 is _____ past 3.

11. Half of €1 is ☐ c.

12. How many $\frac{1}{4}$ litre cartons of cream are needed to make a cake that needs 1 litre of cream? ☐

13. The 12th month of the year is _____ .

14. (70 – 20) + 10 = ☐

15. A can of beans is in the shape of a _____ .

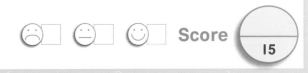 Score ☐ / 15

Work it out!

THURSDAY – WEEK 22

T A B L E S

1. 2 + 4 = ☐
2. 12 – 2 = ☐
3. 2 + 6 = ☐
4. 2 + 1 = ☐
5. 8 + 2 = ☐

6. Emma had 12c. She gave $\frac{1}{2}$ to Rayhan. How much did she give him? ☐ c

7. 12 + 8 = 6 + ☐

8. How many wheels are there on 5 cars? ☐

9. €2 – 50c = € ☐

10. There are ☐ c in €1.

11. Name a shape that has two lines of symmetry. _____

12. How many months are there in two years? ☐

13. Ring the heaviest. $\frac{1}{2}$ kg 1 kg $\frac{1}{4}$ kg

14. How many faces? ☐

15. $\frac{1}{2}$ litre = ☐ millilitres

 Score ☐ / 15

T A B L E S

1. 3 + 3 = ☐
2. 3 + 2 = ☐
3. 8 − 3 = ☐
4. 6 + 3 = ☐
5. 9 − 3 = ☐

6. Caoimhe ate 10 of her 15 sweets. How many has she left? ☐

7. ☐ is $\frac{1}{2}$ of 16.

8. Use the width of your finger to estimate the width of this book. ☐ cm

9. 12 + 6 + ☐ = 25

10. Con has 23 sweets. He needs ☐ more to have 50.

11. 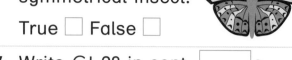 What time is it? It is _____.

12. $\frac{1}{4}$ of 20c is ☐ c.

13. A butterfly is a symmetrical insect. True ☐ False ☐

14. Write €1·28 in cent. ☐ c

15. 1 less than 190 is ☐.

😞 ☐ 😐 ☐ 🙂 ☐ Score ⊘ 15

Work it out!

1. 5 − 3 = **2**
2. 9 + 3 = **12**
3. 11 − 3 = **8**
4. 4 − 3 = **1**
5. 3 + 3 = **6**
6. 3 + 10 = **13**
7. 10 − 3 = **7**
8. 6 − 3 = **13**
9. 3 + 2 = **5**
10. 4 + 3 = **7**
11. 9 − 3 = **6**

12. 7 − 3 = **4**
13. 3 + 0 = **3**
14. 7 + 3 = **10**
15. 5 + 3 = **8**
16. 8 − 3 = **15**
17. 3 + 6 = **9**
18. 3 + 8 = **11**
19. 13 − 3 = **10**
20. 12 − 3 = **9**

😞 ☐ 😐 ☐ 🙂 ☐ Score ⊘ 20

TABLES

1. 3 + 10 = ☐
2. 9 + 3 = ☐
3. 10 − 3 = ☐
4. 3 + 0 = ☐
5. 12 − 3 = ☐

6. `11:00` is _____ o'clock.

7. Tariq has 40c more than Maria. If Maria has 70c, how much has Tariq? ☐ c

8. Colour $\frac{1}{4}$ of the 16 stars. ☆☆☆☆☆☆☆☆ ☆☆☆☆☆☆☆☆

9. 100 − 1 = ☐

10. (<, >, =) 9 + 7 ☐ 20 − 3

11. 20 + 10 + 9 = ☐

12. A _____ is in the shape of a cuboid.

13. Complete this symmetrical shape.

14. If $\frac{1}{2}$ litre of milk is 51c, how much does 1 litre cost? € ☐

15. $\frac{1}{4}$ of 12 is ☐.

 Score ☐☐☐ ／15

Work it out

TABLES

1. 3 + 8 = ☐
2. 4 − 3 = ☐
3. 4 + 3 = ☐
4. 3 + 7 = ☐
5. 3 + 0 = ☐

6. True or false: A pencil is symmetrical. _____

7. Write half past 6 on the digital clock. ☐ : ☐

8. Four $\frac{1}{2}$ kg bags of sugar together weigh ☐ kg.

9. There are ☐ days in June.

10. €2 − €1 − 50c = ☐ c

11. $\frac{1}{4}$ of 16 is ☐.

12. 50c + 50c + 50c + 10c = € ☐

13. 8 is $\frac{1}{2}$ of ☐.

14. How long? (Use a ruler.) ☐ cm

15. A fish tank contains 20 l of water. How many 2 l jugs of water are needed to fill it? ☐

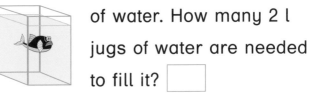
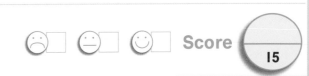 Score ☐☐☐ ／15

TABLES

1. 4 + 4 = ☐
2. 4 + 0 = ☐
3. 6 – 4 = ☐
4. 4 + 8 = ☐
5. 11 – 4 = ☐

6. ☐ There are ☐ lines of symmetry in a square.

7. What is 12 more than 6? ☐

8. 10 + 2 = ☐ + 8

9. How long? (Use a ruler.) ☐ cm

10. **11:30** is half past ☐ .

11. (3 + 15) + 10 = ☐

12. 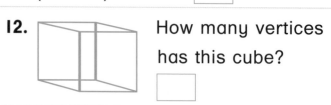 How many vertices has this cube? ☐

13. 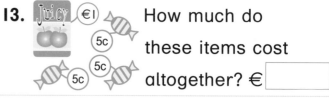 How much do these items cost altogether? € ☐

14. A litre of milk costs 80c. How much does $\frac{1}{2}$ litre cost? ☐ c

15. ($\frac{1}{4}$ of 12) + ($\frac{1}{2}$ of 8) = ☐

 Score ☐ / 15

Work it out.

1. 12 – 4 = ☐
2. 4 + 7 = ☐
3. 7 – 4 = ☐
4. 5 – 4 = ☐
5. 4 + 0 = ☐
6. 2 + 4 = ☐
7. 6 – 4 = ☐
8. 9 – 4 = ☐
9. 5 + 4 = ☐
10. 4 + 4 = ☐
11. 8 – 4 = ☐

12. 13 – 4 = ☐
13. 4 + 10 = ☐
14. 4 + 8 = ☐
15. 4 + 9 = ☐
16. 14 – 4 = ☐
17. 8 + 4 = ☐
18. 4 + 6 = ☐
19. 10 – 4 = ☐
20. 11 – 4 = ☐

 Score ☐ / 20

50

TABLES

1. 4 + 5 =
2. 2 + 4 =
3. 12 − 4 =
4. 4 + 8 =
5. 8 − 4 =

6. How many days in 4 weeks?

7. I have €2. I buy three 20c sweets and a 50c lollipop. How much have I got left? ___ c

8. Colour $\frac{1}{4}$ of the 20 eggs.

9. What is 22c more than 60c? ___ c

10. Add the even numbers.
    1, 2, 3, 4, 5, 6

11. ___ I have ___ lines of symmetry.

12. 5 + 6 + 2 = 4 + ___

13. How many corners?

14. How many $\frac{1}{4}$ litres are needed to fill a 2 litre jug?

15. What is 12 more than 14?

Score ___ / 15

Work it out.

TABLES

1. 4 + 1 =
2. 12 − 4 =
3. 4 + 3 =
4. 4 + 2 =
5. 4 + 6 =

6. 50c more than €1·20 is € ___ .

7. (<, >, =) 20 − 10 ___ 15 − 2

8. How much liquid is in the jug? ___ l

9. What time is 2 hours before 3 o'clock? ___ o'clock

10. How many hours in a day? ___

11. The wafer in a 99 ice-cream is in the shape of a _____ .

12. Add the odd numbers.
    1, 2, 3, 4, 5, 6, 7 ___

13. Fill in the missing numbers.
    186, 187, 188, ___ , ___

14. (12 + 15) + ___ = 30

15. There are 60 cows and 44 sheep on a farm. How many more cows than sheep are there? ___

Score ___ / 15

TABLES

1. 5 + 4 =
2. 2 + 5 =
3. 8 – 5 =
4. 5 + 7 =
5. 12 – 5 =

6. 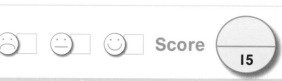 How much? €

7. $\frac{1}{2}$ of 60 cm = 30 cm

8. 1000 ml = 1 l

9. $\frac{1}{2}$ of 50 cm = cm

10. What is 8 less than 20?

11. is $\frac{1}{4}$ of 20.

12. 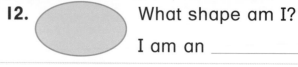 What shape am I? I am an _____ .

13.  I am symmetrical. True ☐ False ☐

14. 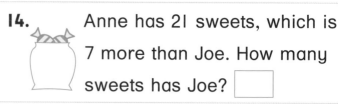 Anne has 21 sweets, which is 7 more than Joe. How many sweets has Joe?

15. Write half past 12 on the digital clock.
☐ : ☐

☹ ☐ 😐 ☐ ☺ ☐ Score 15

Work it out!

1. 13 – 5 =
2. 2 + 5 =
3. 8 – 5 =
4. 5 – 5 =
5. 5 + 5 =
6. 5 + 4 =
7. 10 – 5 =
8. 7 – 5 =
9. 5 + 9 =
10. 5 + 8 =
11. 15 – 5 =

12. 11 – 5 =
13. 5 + 10 =
14. 7 + 5 =
15. 6 + 5 =
16. 12 – 5 =
17. 5 + 0 =
18. 5 + 3 =
19. 9 – 5 =
20. 14 – 5 =

   Score 20

52

WEDNESDAY – WEEK 25

T A B L E S

1. 5 + 6 = ☐
2. 5 + 5 = ☐
3. 9 – 5 = ☐
4. 3 + 5 = ☐
5. 15 – 5 = ☐

6. How much for ten 20c bars?

   € 2

7. How many hours in two days?

   48

8. How many $\frac{1}{4}$ litres of milk are needed to fill a 2 litre jug? ☐

9. 56 + 19 = ☐

10.  Is this a right angle?

    Yes ☐ No ☐

11. 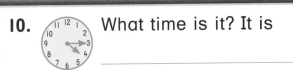 36c — How much change will I get from 50c? 14 c

12. ✓ $\frac{1}{2}$ kg turnips weigh 3 kg.

13. 5 + 5 + 5 + 5 + 5 = ☐

14.  4c — How much for 6? ☐ c

15. Bart has 15c less than Claire. Claire has 30c. How much has Bart? ☐ c

☹ ☐ 😐 ☐ 😊 ☐ Score ⊘ / 15

Work it out!

THURSDAY – WEEK 25

T A B L E S

1. 5 + 10 = ☐
2. 5 – 5 = ☐
3. 8 + 5 = ☐
4. 5 + 7 = ☐
5. 5 + 3 = ☐

6. Write 114c using the € symbol.

   ☐

7. Which has the smaller area? ☐ ☐

8. 20 – 10 = 5 + ☐

9. What is the sum of 20 and 19? ☐

10.  What time is it? It is _____ .

11. Take 15 from 25. ☐

12. Colour the odd one out.

13. $\frac{1}{2}$ of €2 = ☐ c

14. **K** I am symmetrical?

    True ☐ False ☐

15. Fill in the missing numbers.

    3, 13 23, ☐ , ☐ , 53

☹ ☐ 😐 ☐ 😊 ☐ Score ⊘ / 15

MONDAY – WEEK 26

TABLES

1. $6 + 0 =$ ☐
2. $6 + 4 =$ ☐
3. $9 - 6 =$ ☐
4. $8 + 6 =$ ☐
5. $13 - 6 =$ ☐

6. If I spend $\frac{1}{2}$ of €1·40, I will get ☐ c change.

7. Naomi should measure the length of her bed with a metre stick ☐ a ruler ☐.

8. $\frac{1}{2}$ of 24 is ☐.

9. June is the ☐ th month.

10. $(<, >, =)$ $5 + 12$ ☐ $10 + 3$

11. $\frac{1}{4}$ kg bag of flour weighs more ☐ less ☐ than $\frac{1}{2}$ kg bag of flour.

12. 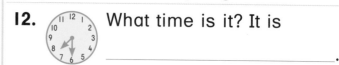 What time is it? It is _____.

13. Paula's book has 35 pages. She read 20 pages. How many pages has she left to read? ☐

14. $27c = €$ ☐

15. A sphere has ☐ face(s).

☹ ☐ 😐 ☐ ☺ ☐ Score ☐ 15

Work it out

TABLES TUESDAY – WEEK 26

1. $16 - 6 =$ ☐
2. $6 + 5 =$ ☐
3. $12 - 6 =$ ☐
4. $10 - 6 =$ ☐
5. $6 + 3 =$ ☐
6. $7 + 6 =$ ☐
7. $14 - 6 =$ ☐
8. $11 - 6 =$ ☐
9. $6 + 4 =$ ☐
10. $6 + 1 =$ ☐
11. $7 - 6 =$ ☐

12. $15 - 6 =$ ☐
13. $10 + 6 =$ ☐
14. $0 + 6 =$ ☐
15. $6 + 9 =$ ☐
16. $8 - 6 =$ ☐
17. $6 + 8 =$ ☐
18. $6 + 6 =$ ☐
19. $9 - 6 =$ ☐
20. $13 - 6 =$ ☐

☹ ☐ 😐 ☐ ☺ ☐ Score ☐ 20

WEDNESDAY – WEEK 26

T A B L E S

1. 6 + 10 = ☐
2. 6 + 0 = ☐
3. 16 – 6 = ☐
4. 6 + 6 = ☐
5. 11 – 6 = ☐

6. 20 + 22 = ☐ + 30

7. $\frac{1}{4}$ of ☐ c is 4c.

8. There are ☐ months in winter.

9. Jane is 5 years older than Ahmed. If Ahmed is 10 years old, how old is Jane? ☐

10. 90 – 40 = ☐

11. Tick which is heavier.
teacher's desk ☐ a chair ☐

12. I am a 3D shape with only 2 faces. I am a _____.

13. 55c less than €1 is ☐ c

14. A spoon is symmetrical.
True ☐ False ☐

15. Joe should measure the height of his wardrobe with a metre stick ☐ a ruler ☐.

 Score ⊘ 15

Work it out

THURSDAY – WEEK 26

T A B L E S

1. 4 + 6 = ☐
2. 6 – 6 = ☐
3. 6 + 6 = ☐
4. 6 + 8 = ☐
5. 6 + 0 = ☐

6. 1c = € ☐

7. How many legs have 3 dogs and 2 cats altogether? ☐

8. $\frac{1}{4}$ litre of yoghurt costs 20c. How much for 1 litre? ☐ c

9. Which holds more? ☐ ☐

10. How many lines of symmetry? ☐

11. Show half past six.

12. $\frac{1}{4}$ of 20 is ☐.

13. 2 + 6 + 7 = ☐

14. Colour half of this triangle.

15. 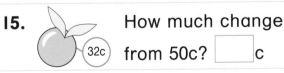 32c How much change from 50c? ☐ c

   Score 15

☞ Page 78 for Friday Test – Week 26.

TABLES

1. 7 + 0 = ☐
2. 3 + 7 = ☐
3. 10 – 7 = ☐
4. 7 + 6 = ☐
5. 15 – 7 = ☐

6. Ring the letters that are symmetrical. L M N O P

7. The sum of 25 and 10 is ☐ .

8. October is the ☐ th month of the year.

9. Start at 60, go back 20 and then forward 5. I am at ☐ .

10. What time is three hours before 9 o'clock? ☐ o'clock

11. A fish tank holds 12 l of water when full. How many litres does it hold when $\frac{1}{2}$ full? ☐ l

12. How many days in July? ☐

13. How long? (Use a ruler.) ☐ cm

14. 12 + ☐ + 5 = 30

15. €2 – €1 – 50c – 20c = ☐ c

 Score ☐ / 15

Work it out

1. 9 – 7 = ☐
2. 1 + 7 = ☐
3. 13 – 7 = ☐
4. 10 – 7 = ☐
5. 7 + 2 = ☐
6. 7 + 4 = ☐
7. 8 – 7 = ☐
8. 16 – 7 = ☐
9. 7 + 3 = ☐
10. 7 + 10 = ☐
11. 15 – 7 = ☐

12. 17 – 7 = ☐
13. 7 + 7 = ☐
14. 7 + 9 = ☐
15. 5 + 7 = ☐
16. 12 – 7 = ☐
17. 6 + 7 = ☐
18. 7 + 8 = ☐
19. 11 – 7 = ☐
20. 14 – 7 = ☐

   Score / 20

T A B L E S

1. $6 + 7 =$ ☐
2. $7 + 5 =$ ☐
3. $17 - 7 =$ ☐
4. $7 + 9 =$ ☐
5. $13 - 7 =$ ☐

6. €1·52 =
   €1 + 20c + ☐ c + 10c + 2c

7. I am a symmetrical shape with four equal sides. I am a _____.

8. €1·65 = ☐ c

9. ($<$, $>$, $=$) $\frac{1}{2}$ of 12 ☐ $\frac{1}{4}$ of 8

10. When it is 9:30, it is _____ past 9.

11. ☐ $- 6 = 10$

12. My bed is longer ☐ shorter ☐ than 1 metre.

13. $5 + 8 = 6 +$ ☐

14. Show 9 o'clock.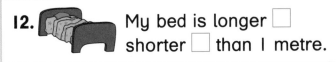

15. Between both of them Emma and Jamie have €1·60. If Jamie has 9c, how much money has Emma?
    € ☐

☹ ☐ ☺ ☐ ☺ ☐ Score ☐/15

Work it out

T A B L E S

1. $7 + 4 =$ ☐
2. $13 - 7 =$ ☐
3. $7 + 0 =$ ☐
4. $5 + 7 =$ ☐
5. $6 + 7 =$ ☐

6. Leah is 8 years younger than Michael. If Michael is 12, how old is Leah? ☐

7. Five children have ☐ toes altogether.

8. 196, 197, ☐ , ☐

9. € ☐ = 71c

10. Estimate the length of your pencil. ☐ cm

11. $(3 + 5) +$ ☐ $= 20$

12. I can roll, stack and slide. I am a _____.

13. A fish tank holds 10 cm ☐, 10 l ☐, 10 kg ☐ of water.

14.  $\frac{1}{4}$ of 40c is ☐ c.

15.  What time is it? It is _____.

☹ ☐ ☺ ☐ ☺ ☐ Score ☐/15

TABLES

1. 8 + 3 = ☐
2. 8 + 2 = ☐
3. 12 – 8 = ☐
4. 7 + 8 = ☐
5. 18 – 8 = ☐

6. 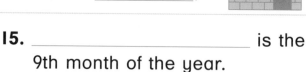 How much? € ☐

7. A T-shirt is a symmetrical item of clothing. Yes ☐ No ☐

8.  $\frac{1}{4}$ of 80c is ☐ c.

9. 30 + 20 = 10 + ☐

10. $1\frac{1}{2}$ m = ☐ cm

11. A bath holds 80 litres of water. It holds ☐ l when $\frac{1}{2}$ full.

12. Take 40 from 50. ☐

13. $\frac{1}{2}$ m = ☐ cm

14. I am a 3D shape used in walls. I am a _____ .

15. _____ is the 9th month of the year.

☹ ☐ ☺ ☐ 😊 ☐ Score ◯ 15

Work it out

1. 15 – 8 = ☐
2. 6 + 8 = ☐
3. 16 – 8 = ☐
4. 13 – 8 = ☐
5. 8 + 1 = ☐
6. 8 + 7 = ☐
7. 17 – 8 = ☐
8. 14 – 8 = ☐
9. 8 + 5 = ☐
10. 8 + 0 = ☐
11. 18 – 8 = ☐

12. 8 – 8 = ☐
13. 8 + 8 = ☐
14. 8 + 4 = ☐
15. 9 + 8 = ☐
16. 12 – 8 = ☐
17. 8 + 3 = ☐
18. 10 + 8 = ☐
19. 11 – 8 = ☐
20. 10 – 8 = ☐

☹ ☐ ☺ ☐ 😊 ☐ Score ◯ 20

WEDNESDAY – WEEK 28

TABLES

1. 8 + 4 = ☐
2. 5 + 8 = ☐
3. 10 – 8 = ☐
4. 2 + 8 = ☐
5. 13 – 8 = ☐

6. €1·21 = ☐ c
7. ☐ is 12 more than 20.
8. What is 15 less than 30? ☐
9. (<, >, =) 13 + 1 ☐ 12 + 2
10. What seven coins make up 65c?

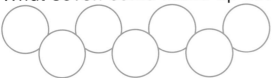

11. Add 26 to 20. ☐
12. Tick which holds more. ☐ ☐
13. Write half past 8 on the digital clock. ☐ :
14. Five 30c apples cost € ☐ .

30c

15. 1 m + ½ m = ☐ cm

☹ ☐ ☺ ☐ ☺ ☐ Score ☐ / 15

Work it out!

THURSDAY – WEEK 28

TABLES

1. 8 + 10 = ☐
2. 12 – 8 = ☐
3. 8 + 2 = ☐
4. 8 + 8 = ☐
5. 6 + 8 = ☐

6. ☐ How many lines of symmetry? ☐

7. Billy won a silver medal. He came ☐ nd in the race.

8. How much more than €1·45 is €2? ☐ c

9. 40 + 20 + ☐ = 75

10. 109 = ☐ hundred, ☐ tens and ☐ units

11. Which 3 coins make up €1·60? ◯ ◯ ◯

12. Write a quarter to 5 on the digital clock. ☐ :

13. ◗ I am a _____ .

14. (½ of 40) + (¼ of 8) = ☐

15. ☐ is 3rd in the alphabet.

☹ ☐ ☺ ☐ ☺ ☐ Score ☐ / 15

MONDAY – WEEK 29

TABLES

1. 9 + 3 =
2. 9 + 5 =
3. 12 – 9 =
4. 7 + 9 =
5. 19 – 9 =

6. Colour $\frac{1}{4}$ of the circle.

7. 50c + 50c + 50c + 20c + ⬚ c + ⬚ c = €2

8. _____ is the 8th month of the year.

9. What is 45 more than 10? ⬚

10.  How much? € ⬚

11.  It is $\frac{1}{4}$ ____ 8.

12. Which has the greater area?  ⬚ ⬚

13. What is the value of 3 in 139? ⬚

14.  How many faces has a cone? ⬚

15. (+, –) 100 ⬚ 20 = 80

☹ ⬚ 😐 ⬚ ☺ ⬚ Score **15**

Work it out

TABLES TUESDAY – WEEK 29

1. 15 – 9 =
2. 9 + 1 =
3. 11 – 9 =
4. 17 – 9 =
5. 9 + 5 =
6. 10 + 9 =
7. 12 – 9 =
8. 16 – 9 =
9. 9 + 9 =
10. 9 + 6 =
11. 19 – 9 =

12. 13 – 9 =
13. 3 + 9 =
14. 9 + 8 =
15. 9 + 4 =
16. 14 – 9 =
17. 9 + 2 =
18. 9 + 7 =
19. 9 – 9 =
20. 18 – 9 =

☹ ⬚ 😐 ⬚ ☺ ⬚ Score **20**

WEDNESDAY – WEEK 29

TABLES

1. $9 + 0 =$ ☐
2. $9 + 3 =$ ☐
3. $17 - 9 =$ ☐
4. $5 + 9 =$ ☐
5. $9 - 9 =$ ☐

6. How many tiles are needed to cover the table? ☐

7. There were 31 children in a class. 6 girls left. How many girls are there if there are 13 boys? ☐

8. $(12 + 8 + 6) = (10 + $ ☐ $)$

9. $(\frac{1}{2}$ of 12$) + (\frac{1}{2}$ of 8$) =$ ☐

10. $50c + $ ☐ $c = €2$

11. $154 = $ ☐ hundred, ☐ tens and ☐ units

12. What is the 4th letter in MATHS? ☐

13. A ball is in the shape of a _____.

14. Write the number between 158 and 160. ☐

15. How many lines of symmetry. ☐

 Score ☐☐☐ ⊘/15

Work it out

THURSDAY – WEEK 29

TABLES

1. $9 + 1 =$ ☐
2. $12 - 9 =$ ☐
3. $9 + 0 =$ ☐
4. $9 + 5 =$ ☐
5. $9 + 8 =$ ☐

6. Oisín has €2. He buys two 5c lollies and a 50c comic. What change will he get? ☐

7. $4 + 4 + 4 + 4 + 4 =$ ☐

8. What is 15 less than 100? ☐

9. How long? (Use a ruler.) ☐ cm

10. Tara is 16. John is 5 years older. How old is John? ☐

11. `09:30` This clock is 2 hours fast. Write the correct time. ☐ : ☐

12. $45 + 31 =$ ☐

13. Fill in the missing numbers.
    12, 16, 20, ☐, 28, ☐

14. $(+, -)$ 19 ☐ 17 $= 2$

15. How many legs altogether have 3 dogs and 2 chickens? ☐

 Score ☐☐☐ ⊘/15

T A B L E S

1. 10 + 4 = ☐
2. 10 + 1 = ☐
3. 18 – 10 = ☐
4. 10 + 8 = ☐
5. 17 – 10 = ☐

6. 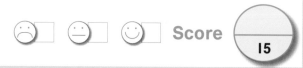 = ☐

7. Write 3 hours after 6:30 on the digital clock. ☐ : ☐

8. 62 – 11 = ☐

9. How many $\frac{1}{4}$ kg blocks of butter are needed to make 1 kg? ☐

10. (32 – 5) + 6 = ☐

11. $\frac{1}{4}$ of ☐ = 4

12. 105 = ☐ hundred, ☐ tens and ☐ units

13. What shape am I? I am a _____.

14. True or false: A cylinder can roll and be stacked. _____

15. I have 3 boxes of 6 eggs. How many eggs have I? ☐

☹ ☐ 😐 ☐ ☺ ☐ Score ⊘ 15

Work it out

1. 16 – 10 = ☐
2. 8 + 10 = ☐
3. 15 – 10 = ☐
4. 13 – 10 = ☐
5. 10 + 2 = ☐
6. 10 + 3 = ☐
7. 20 – 10 = ☐
8. 14 – 10 = ☐
9. 10 + 1 = ☐
10. 10 + 7 = ☐
11. 19 – 10 = ☐

12. 17 – 10 = ☐
13. 5 + 10 = ☐
14. 10 + 0 = ☐
15. 6 + 10 = ☐
16. 10 – 10 = ☐
17. 10 + 10 = ☐
18. 4 + 10 = ☐
19. 18 – 10 = ☐
20. 12 – 10 = ☐

☹ ☐ 😐 ☐ ☺ ☐ Score ⊘ 20

WEDNESDAY – WEEK 30

T A B L E S

1. 7 + 10 = ☐
2. 10 + 2 = ☐
3. 14 − 10 = ☐
4. 10 + 4 = ☐
5. 12 − 10 = ☐

6. (+, −) 25 ☐ 3 = 22

7. Draw the other half of this house.

8. $\frac{1}{2}$ of a 30 cm ruler is ☐ cm.

9. = ☐

10. (23 + 20) − 4 = ☐

11. I had €1·50. I spent 60c. I have ☐ left.

12. The are ☐ months in a season.

13. Show noon on the digital clock.

14. Which is heavier?  ☐ ☐

15. How many $\frac{1}{4}$ l cartons of juice are needed to fill a 1 $\frac{1}{2}$ l jug? ☐

😞 ☐ 😐 ☐ 🙂 ☐ Score ―/15

Work it out!

THURSDAY – WEEK 30

T A B L E S

1. 10 + 5 = ☐
2. 19 − 10 = ☐
3. 10 + 1 = ☐
4. 10 + 2 = ☐
5. 3 + 10 = ☐

6. (<, >, =) 3 + 12 ☐ 6 + 8

7. How many right angles? ☐

8. 8, 12, 16, ☐, ☐, 28, ☐

9. This is the ☐ th flower.

10. (+, −) 40 ☐ 24 = 64

11. Which is bigger: $\frac{1}{4}$ of the cake or $\frac{1}{2}$ of the cake? ☐

12. If I subtract 12 from 24, the answer is ☐.

13. Which shape is divided in $\frac{1}{4}$s? ☐ ☐

14. 187, 188, 189, ☐

15. Sam puts four 5c stamps on his letter. How much did the four stamps cost? ☐ c

😞 ☐ 😐 ☐ 🙂 ☐ Score ―/15

☞ Page 80 for Friday Test – Week 30.

64

FRIDAY TESTS

FRIDAY TESTS

WEEK 1

1. What time is it?
   a 12 o'clock b 6 o'clock
   ✓ 5 o'clock

2. $\frac{1}{2}$ of 6 is ☐. a 12 ⓑ 3 c 8

3. The 3 in 37 = ☐
   a 3 b 13 c 30

4. A triangle has ☐ sides.
   ⓐ 3 b 4 c 5

5. How many legs have two dogs?
   a 2 b 4 ⓒ 8

6. ____ is the 2nd month of the year.
   a January ⓑ February c April

7. ☐ is 4 more than 6.
   a 2 ⓑ 10 c 9

8. 10c + 10c + 10c + 5c = ☐ c

   ⓐ 35 b 25 c 80

9. What is the missing number?
   2, 4, 6, 8, ☐   a 11 b 9 ⓒ 10

10. 10 + 1 = ☐ ⓐ 11 b 9 c 12

☹ ☐ 😐 ☐ ☺ ☐ Score ─── / 10

WEEK 2

1.  Which is heavier?
   a bicycle b pencil
   c stool

2. 6**4** The underlined number has a value of ☐.
   a 4 b 40 c 400

3. There are ☐ days in a week.
   a 5 b 6 c 7

4. It is ☐ o'clock.
   a 5 b 12 c 7

5. (4 + 2) + 3 = ☐
   a 6 b 9 c 3

6. What is the missing number?
   3, ☐, 7, 9, 11
   a 1 b 5 c 4

7. $\frac{1}{2}$ of 40 is ☐. a 20 b 10 c 80

8. A rectangle has ☐ sides.
   a 2 b 4 c 6

9.
   = ☐ tens and ☐ units
   a 1 ten, 5 units b 6 units
   c 15 units

10. 20c + 15c = ☐ c a 5 b 30 c 35

☹ ☐ 😐 ☐ ☺ ☐ Score ─── / 10

Work it out

66

FRIDAY TESTS

WEEK 3

1. ☐ of this shape is coloured. ⓐ $\frac{1}{2}$ ⓑ $\frac{1}{4}$ ⓒ $\frac{1}{8}$

2. $10c + 5c + 2c + 1c =$ ☐ c
   ⓐ 37 ⓑ 18 ⓒ 17

3. $25 - 10 =$ ☐ ⓐ 35 ⓑ 10 ⓒ 15

4. It is ☐ o'clock.
   ⓐ 3 ⓑ 9 ⓒ 12

5. Which is longer?
   ⓐ brush ⓑ ladder
   ⓒ both the same

6. = ☐ tens and ☐ units
   ⓐ 3 tens, 8 units
   ⓑ 8 tens, 3 units
   ⓒ 11 units

7. $\frac{1}{2}$ of 10 is ☐. ⓐ 20 ⓑ 5 ⓒ 2

8. Which holds more?
   ⓐ eggcup ⓑ bottle cap
   ⓒ both the same

9. A ball is in the shape of a _____.
   ⓐ cube ⓑ sphere ⓒ cone

10. Christmas is in the month of ____.
    ⓐ January ⓑ May ⓒ December

 ☐ ☐  ☐ Score 10

WEEK 4

1. 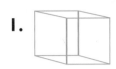 A cube has ☐ faces.
   ⓐ 4 ⓑ 6 ⓒ 8

2. What is double 20?
   ⓐ 40 ⓑ 10 ⓒ 30

3. ☐ 10c coins are needed to make 50c. ⓐ 10 ⓑ 5 ⓒ 6

4. $10 + 6 =$ ☐ $+ 1$
   ⓐ 16 ⓑ 17 ⓒ 15

5. $\frac{1}{2}$ of ☐ is 10. ⓐ 5 ⓑ 10 ⓒ 20

6. 2, 4, 6 and 8 are all _____ numbers. ⓐ odd ⓑ even ⓒ big

7. The winner is the person who comes _____. ⓐ 1st ⓑ 2nd ⓒ 3rd

8. What time is it?
   ⓐ $\frac{1}{2}$ past 3 ⓑ $\frac{1}{2}$ past 4
   ⓒ 4 o'clock

9. 40, 50, 60, ☐, 80
   ⓐ 70 ⓑ 90 ⓒ 60

10. There are ☐ days in January.
    ⓐ 29 ⓑ 30 ⓒ 31

 ☐ ☐ ☐ Score 10

Work it out

FRIDAY TESTS

WEEK 5

1.  Which holds more?
☐a jug ☐b cup ☑c bucket

2. ☐ is double 40. ☑a 20 ☐b 40 ☐c 80

3. What shape am I?
☐a sphere ☐b cone
☑c cube

4. 40c + 20c = ☐
☐a 60c ☑b 80c ☐c 20c

5. What is 10 less than 20?
☐a 30 ☑b 10 ☐c 20

6. What number is one before 20?
☐a 10 ☑b 19 ☐c 21

7. Which is heavier?
☐a feather ☐b sock ☑c book

8. 10 ☐ 9 ☑a < ☐b > ☐c =

9. ☐ is ½ of 10. ☐a 10 ☑b 5 ☐c 20

10. Five monkeys have two bananas each. How many bananas altogether?
☐a 5 ☑b 10 ☐c 7

☹ ☐ 😐 ☐ 🙂 ☐ Score ─── /10

WEEK 6

1. 10 − 6 = ☐ ☐a 2 ☑b 4 ☐c 8

2. A square has ☐ square corners.
☐a 2 ☐b 3 ☑c 4

3. This shape is a/an _____.
☐a oval ☑b circle ☐c sphere

4. ½ of 16 is ☐. ☑a 8 ☐b 32 ☐c 14

5. What time is it?
☐a ½ past 6 ☑b ¼ past 6
☐c ½ past 3

6. A _____ weighs less than 1 kg.
☐a car ☐b table ☑c magazine

7. There are ☐ minutes in 1 hour.
☐a 6 ☐b 100 ☑c 60

8. 10c + 10c + ☐c = 25c
☑a 5 ☐b 10 ☐c 20

9. A triangle has ☐ corners.
☐a 1 ☑b 3 ☐c 4

10. ☐ = ☐ tens and ☐ units
☑a 3 tens, 0 units
☐b 3 tens, 3 units
☐c 33 tens, 0 units

☹ ☐ 😐 ☐ 🙂 ☐ Score ─── /10

Work it out.

FRIDAY TESTS

WEEK 7

1. ☐ is ½ of 12. ☐a 6 ☐b 24 ✓ ☐c 20

2. There are ☐ months in a year.
☐a 10 ☐b 60 ☐c 12 ✓

3. A bucket of water is measured in
_____. ☐a metres ☐b litres ✓
☐c kilograms

4. 24 + 9 = ☐ ☐a 35 ☐b 33 ✓ ☐c 34

5. 18 less 6 is ☐. ☐a 12 ✓ ☐b 24 ☐c 10

6. 5 tens and 7 units is ☐.
☐a 57 ✓ ☐b 75 ☐c 12

7. I am a _____.
☐a cone ☐b cube ✓ ☐c sphere

8. It is _____.
☐a ¼ past 9 ☐b ¼ to 3 ✓
☐c ½ past 9

9. Who is taller?
☐a Tom ☐b Joe
☐ both the same ✓

Tom   Joe

10. This page is approximately ☐
pens long. ☐a 2 ✓ ☐b 5 ✓ ☐c 10

😞 ☐ 😐 ☐ 🙂 ☐ Score ── /10

WEEK 8

1. I am a flat shape with four sides.
What am I?
☐a circle ☐b triangle ☐c square

2. 20 shared between two is ☐
each. ☐a 40 ☐b 10 ☐c 80

3. ☐ 20c coins make €1.
☐a 10 ☐b 3 ☐c 5

4. I have ☐ square corners.
☐a 2 ☐b 3 ☐c 4

5. 6 + 10 = ☐ + 4 ☐a 6 ☐b 20 ☐c 12

6. If today is Saturday, tomorrow
will be _____.
☐a Monday ☐b Sunday ☐c Friday

7. A _____ weighs about 1 kg.
☐a bag of flour ☐b pencil ☐c chair

8. 5 chairs at each of 4 tables. How
many chairs? ☐a 10 ☐b 20 ☐c 9

9. ¼ of 8 is ☐. ☐a 2 ☐b 4 ☐c 8

10. 50 less 30 is ☐. ☐a 20 ☐b 30 ☐c 40

😞 ☐ 😐 ☐ 🙂 ☐ Score ── /10

Work it out

FRIDAY TESTS

1. Which is the odd one out?
   a triangle b circle c cube

2. 100 cm = 1 ___
   a m b kg c cm

3. This shape has ☐ square corners. a 2 b 3 c 5

4. Three dogs have ☐ legs altogether. a 8 b 10 c 12

5. ☐ + 10 = 18 a 28 b 8 c 2

6. What time will it be in half an hour? a $\frac{1}{2}$ past 6 b $\frac{1}{2}$ past 7 c 7 o'clock

7. Who is 2nd? a Mary b Tom c Jess
   Mary Tom Jess

8. How many days are there in three weeks? a 7 b 14 c 21

9. How much? 10c 30c a 30c b 50c c 40c

10. 12 is ☐ more than 3. a 15 b 9 c 6

☹ ☐ 😐 ☐ ☺ ☐ Score 10

1. A bath holds ___. a 1 l b more than 1 l c less than 1 l

2. How many 10c coins make €1? a 10 b 1 c 100

3. How many minutes in half an hour? a 60 b 15 c 30

4. $\frac{1}{2}$ m + $\frac{1}{2}$ m = ☐ m a $\frac{1}{4}$ m b 1 m c 50 cm

5. 40 + ☐ = 65 a 105 b 25 c 50

6. 163 = 1 hundred, ☐ tens and 3 units. a 6 b 3 c 1

7. How many wheels have 6 bicycles? a 10 b 12 c 8

8. A rectangle has ☐ lines of symmetry a 1 b 2 c 4

9. A jug holds 1 l. Half this jug holds ☐ l. a $\frac{1}{2}$ l b $\frac{1}{4}$ l c 1 l

10. It is $\frac{1}{4}$ to 3. In 1 hour it will be:
    a $\frac{1}{4}$ past 3 b $\frac{1}{4}$ to 5 c $\frac{1}{4}$ to 4

☹ ☐ 😐 ☐ ☺ ☐ Score 10

Work it out

70

FRIDAY TESTS

WEEK 11

1. How many legs have 2 octopuses? [a] 4 [b] 8 [c] 16

2.  I am a _____ . [a] cube [b] cuboid [c] cone

3. Which shape is not symmetrical? [a] ☆ [b] ◺ [c] ▢

4. A cup holds ____ 1 l. [a] exactly [b] more than [c] less than

5. Colour $\frac{1}{2}$. How many sections are coloured? [a] 1 [b] 2 [c] 4

6. If I cut a square in half, I get ____ . [a] circles [b] squares [c] triangles

7. The classroom door is about ▢ m. [a] 1 [b] 2 [c] 5

8. ▢ c + 10c + 5c + 2c = 37c [a] 10 [b] 20 [c] 5

9.  What time was it 1 hour ago? [a] $\frac{1}{4}$ to 10 [b] $\frac{1}{4}$ past 10 [c] $\frac{1}{2}$ past 11

10. ▢ + 8 = 6 + 10 [a] 24 [b] 8 [c] 16

😞▢ 😐▢ 😊▢ Score ⊘ 10

WEEK 12

1. $\frac{1}{4}$ of 8 is ▢. [a] 4 [b] 2 [c] 3

2.  How many square corners inside this shape? [a] 2 [b] 4 [c] 5

3.  How much would four 10c lollipops cost? [a] 20c [b] 30c [c] 40c

4. 2 kg + ▢ kg = 5 kg [a] 1 [b] 3 [c] 5

5. _____ is three days after Monday. [a] Tuesday [b] Thursday [c] Wednesday

6. Which of the following can hold more than 1 litre? [a] cup [b] jug [c] spoon

7. 15 ▢ 3 + 6 + 2 [a] > [b] < [c] =

8. ▢ + 4 = 12 [a] 10 [b] 8 [c] 16

9. 2 o'clock is ▢ : ▢ in digital time. [a] 2:00 [b] 22:00 [c] 20:00

10. Three bottles of water cost €3. How much for one bottle? [a] €1 [b] €3 [c] €2

😞▢ 😐▢ 😊▢ Score ⊘ 10

Work it out

WEEK 13

1. This jug contains ☐ l.
[a] $\frac{1}{4}$ [b] $\frac{1}{2}$ [c] $\frac{3}{4}$

2. My door is about ☐ m.
[a] 2 [b] 3 [c] 4

3. Paul has 8 more sweets than Ciara. Ciara has 10 sweets. How many sweets has Paul?
[a] 2 [b] 18 [c] 20

4. What is 10 more than 64?
[a] 54 [b] 74 [c] 84

5. Abdul coloured $\frac{1}{4}$ of this shape. He coloured ☐ sections. [a] 2 [b] 4 [c] 1

6. 21 + 3 + 4 = ☐   [a] 20 [b] 24 [c] 28

7. There are ☐ months in a year.
[a] 10 [b] 12 [c] 6

8. A cone has ☐ faces.
[a] 2 [b] 3 [c] 4

9. A packet of cards has 6 cards. How many cards in 4 packets?
[a] 20 [b] 24 [c] 10

10. 2 + 12 ☐ 10 − 2 [a] < [b] = [c] >

   Score 10

WEEK 14

1. A school desk is about ☐ metre.
[a] $\frac{1}{2}$ [b] 1 [c] $\frac{1}{4}$

2. A cube has ☐ faces.
[a] 2 [b] 4 [c] 6

3. 40 + 50 = ☐   [a] 90 [b] 100 [c] 10

4. 20c + 50c + 5c + ☐c = 80c
[a] 10 [b] 20 [c] 5

5. 4 + 4 + 4 = ☐   [a] 8 [b] 12 [c] 3

6. Half past nine on a digital clock is ☐. [a] 09:30 [b] 9:12 [c] $\frac{1}{2}$ past 9

7. I had 41 swap cards. I got 11 more. I now have ☐. [a] 51 [b] 50 [c] 52

8. 72 = 30 + 20 + ☐
[a] 22 [b] 12 [c] 2

9. How much change will I get from €2 if I buy a 50c ice-cream?
[a] €1 [b] €1·50 [c] 50c

10. $\frac{1}{4}$ of 12 is ☐. [a] 3 [b] 4 [c] 6

 Score 10

Work it out

FRIDAY TESTS

WEEK 15

1. Christmas Day is the ☐ of December. [a] 1st [b] 25th [c] 31st

2. A star is a _____ shape. [a] symmetrical [b] 3D [c] 4-sided

3. 5 + 5 + 5 + 5 + 5 = ☐ [a] 15 [b] 20 [c] 25

4. Butter ½kg How many are needed to make 1 kg? [a] 1 [b] 2 [c] 4

5. It is _____. [a] $\frac{1}{4}$ past 12 [b] $\frac{1}{4}$ to 11 [c] $\frac{1}{4}$ past 1

6. 10c is ☐ of 20c. [a] $\frac{1}{2}$ [b] $\frac{1}{4}$ [c] $\frac{1}{8}$

7. 20 + 12 = ☐ + 8 [a] 32 [b] 24 [c] 40

8. ☐ $\frac{1}{2}$ ls of water are needed to fill a 3 l jug. [a] 3 [b] 5 [c] 6

9. 6 tens = ☐ [a] 6 [b] 16 [c] 60

10. **06:30** What time is it? [a] $\frac{1}{2}$ past 3 [b] $\frac{1}{4}$ past 6 [c] $\frac{1}{2}$ past 6

☹ ☐ 😐 ☐ ☺ ☐ Score —/10

WEEK 16

1. There are ☐ $\frac{1}{4}$ metres in 1 metre. [a] 2 [b] 4 [c] 5

2. I had €2. I spent half of it. How much do I have left? [a] 50c [b] €1 [c] 20c

3. Two children have ☐ fingers altogether. [a] 5 [b] 10 [c] 20

4. Paula buys two 20c ice-pops and a 50c comic. How much does she spend? [a] 70c [b] 90c [c] 80c

5. There are 30 people on a train. 5 get off and 11 get on. How many are now on the train? [a] 36 [b] 25 [c] 24

6. Which letter is symmetrical? [a] M [b] N [c] F

7. 11 − 3 = ☐ [a] 14 [b] 8 [c] 7

8. 20 + 30 + ☐ = 80 [a] 20 [b] 30 [c] 40

9. A cube has ☐ vertices. [a] 4 [b] 12 [c] 8

10. 9 o'clock is ☐ : ☐ on a digital clock. [a] 9:00 [b] 90:00 [c] 900

☹ ☐ 😐 ☐ ☺ ☐ Score —/10

Work it out

FRIDAY TESTS

WEEK 17

1. $\frac{1}{2}$ past 7 is ☐ : ☐ .
   a 7:30   b 8:30   c 7:20

2. 25 + 6 ☐ 35 – 6   a < b > c =

3. Which of the following is the smallest?   a $\frac{1}{2}$ l   b 1 l   c $\frac{1}{4}$ l

4. $\frac{1}{2}$ of ☐ is 2.   a 2   b 4   c 1

5. This line is ☐ cm long.
   _____
   a 1   b 5   c 10

6. It is _____.
   a $\frac{1}{4}$ past 5   b $\frac{1}{4}$ to 6
   c $\frac{1}{4}$ to 5

7. Tariq ate $\frac{1}{2}$ a bag of sweets. There are four left. How many did he eat?   a 2   b 8   c 4

8. 96, 97, 98, 99, ☐
   a 99   b 10   c 100

9. There are 10 marbles in a bag. How many in three bags?
   a 3   b 30   c 10

10. €2 – €1·50 = ☐
    a 50c   b €2   c €1·50

😞 ☐ 😐 ☐ 🙂 ☐ Score —— 10

WEEK 18

1. I can roll and slide but I cannot be stacked. I am a _____.
   a cube   b cylinder   c cone

2. $\frac{1}{2}$ past 12 is ☐ : ☐ .
   a 12:30   b 30:12   c 12:20

3. $\frac{1}{4}$ of 8 is 2. What is $\frac{2}{4}$ of 8?
   a 2   b 4   c 8

4. A cylinder has ☐ faces.
   a 3   b 2   c 4

5. What is the fewest number of coins needed to make €1·65?
   a 3   b 4   c 5

6. A farmer has 5 dogs, 3 cats, 14 cows and 11 sheep. How many animals has she altogether?
   a 30   b 29   c 33

7. $\frac{1}{2}$ of 10 is ☐.   a 5   b 4   c 8

8. ☐ tens = 90   a 10   b 9   c 8

9. ☐ $\frac{1}{2}$ metres are needed to make 1 m.   a 2   b 3   c 4

10. There are ☐ ml in 1 litre.
    a 10   b 100   c 1000

😞 ☐ 😐 ☐ 🙂 ☐ Score —— 10

Work it out

74

FRIDAY TESTS

WEEK 19

1. Which letter is not symmetrical?

a X b F c E

2. A cuboid has ☐ faces.

a 4 b 6 c 8

3. One hour before 8:30 is ☐.

a 9:30 b 8:30 c 7:30

4. €2 − (50c + 10c) = ☐

a 40c b €1·40 c €1·50

5. There are ☐ cm in 1 metre.

a 100 b 25 c 50

6. $\frac{1}{4}$ of 12 is ☐   a 3 b 4 c 6

7. There are ☐ minutes in half an hour. a 60 b 30 c 15

8. This clock shows _____.
a $\frac{1}{4}$ to 4 b $\frac{1}{4}$ to 3
c $\frac{1}{4}$ past 3

9. How long is this line?

_____

a 3 cm b 5 cm c 7 cm

10. What is the difference between 60 and 30? a 90 b 30 c 20

☹ ☐ 😐 ☐ ☺ ☐ Score ⊘ 10

WEEK 20

1. There are eight stickers in a pack. How many in three packs?

a 8 b 16 c 24

2. Sarah is 15 cm taller than Zac. Zac is 100 cm. How tall is Sarah?

a 115 cm b 85 cm c 125 cm

3. Siobhán has €1.62. How much more does she need to buy a €2 ice-pop? a 48c b 38c c 42c

4. ✓ This face on a cylinder is a/an _____. a oval
b circle c semi-circle

5. (22 + 12) − 9 = ☐ a 25 b 24 c 43

6. $\frac{2}{4}$ of these sweets = ☐.
a 2 b 4 c 8

7. Two 20c pencils, two 12c rubbers and a 10c sharpener cost ☐.
a 74c b 47c c 67c

8. **1̲43** The underlined digit has a value of ☐.
a 4 b 400 c 40

9. $\frac{1}{4}$ kg of sugar costs 50c. How much for 1 kg?
a €1 b €1·50 c €2·00

10. A cube has 6 _____ faces.
a square b rectangle c circle

☹ ☐ 😐 ☐ ☺ ☐ Score ⊘ 10

Work it out

FRIDAY TESTS

WEEK 21

1. 13 less than 30 is ☐.
   [a] 43 [b] 17 [c] 13

2. ☐ $\frac{1}{4}$ l cups of water are needed to fill a 1 l pot. [a] 2 [b] 4 [c] 10

3. 100 = 20 + 50 + ☐
   [a] 30 [b] 20 [c] 40

4. ($\frac{1}{2}$ of 10) + ($\frac{1}{4}$ of 8) = ☐
   [a] 9 [b] 7 [c] 6

5. A funfair ride says you must be 110 cm or taller to go on it. Ethan is 89 cm. How much taller does he need to be?
   [a] 21 cm [b] 31 cm [c] 11 cm

6. ☐ − 20 = 50 [a] 30 [b] 70 [c] 43

7. Which shape is not symmetrical?

8. There are ☐ tens in 1_7_3.
   [a] 1 [b] 7 [c] 3

9. A bucket holds 5 litres. ☐ 1 litre bottles are needed to fill it.
   [a] 10 [b] 5 [c] 3

10. 40 + ☐ + 5 = 95 [a] 40 [b] 45 [c] 50

☹ ☐ 😐 ☐ ☺ ☐ Score ──/10

WEEK 22

1. $\frac{1}{2}$ of 20 is ☐. [a] 40 [b] 10 [c] 5

2. $\frac{1}{4}$ m = ☐ cm. [a] 25 [b] 10 [c] 50

3. What is one less than 100?
   [a] 90 [b] 99 [c] 101

4. ☐ $\frac{1}{2}$ kg bags of sand will fill a pit needing 3 kg. [a] 2 [b] 4 [c] 6

5. A sphere has ☐ corners.
   [a] 0 [b] 1 [c] 2

6. 30 + 5 = ☐ + 10
   [a] 35 [b] 25 [c] 45

7. Which is greatest?
   [a] $\frac{1}{4}$ l [b] $\frac{1}{2}$ l [c] 1 l

8. Which shape has two lines of symmetry?
   [a] rectangle [b] heart [c] triangle

9. The width of your finger is approximately ☐.
   [a] 1 cm [b] 1 m [c] 1 kg

10. How many legs have 6 four-legged chairs? [a] 10 [b] 12 [c] 24

☹ ☐ 😐 ☐ ☺ ☐ Score ──/10

Work it out

76

FRIDAY TESTS

WEEK 23

1. Eibhlín and Orlagh have 45 sweets between them. If Eibhlín has 26 sweets, how many has Orlagh? [a] 20 [b] 19 [c] 71

2. One less than 180 is ☐.
[a] 179 [b] 189 [c] 181

3. (€1 + 50c) − €1·20 = ☐
[a] 30c [b] 40c [c] 50c

4. $\frac{1}{4}$ of ☐ = 4 [a] 8 [b] 1 [c] 16

5. A _____ is the same shape as a cuboid.
[a] cereal box [b] ball [c] die

6. 13 + 12 = 10 + ☐ [a] 25 [b] 35 [c] 15

7. €1 + 50c + 20c + 10c = ☐
[a] €1·70 [b] €1·80 [c] €1·60

8.  What time is two hours later? [a] $\frac{1}{2}$ past 6 [b] $\frac{1}{2}$ past 10 [c] $\frac{1}{2}$ past 9

9. How many $\frac{1}{2}$ l jugs can be filled from a basin containing 8 litres?
[a] 8 [b] 4 [c] 16

10. This line is ☐ cm.

_____
[a] 5 cm [b] 6 cm [c] 7 cm

😞 ☐ 😐 ☐ 🙂 ☐ Score ◯ 10

WEEK 24

1. ($\frac{1}{2}$ of 40) + ($\frac{1}{4}$ of 12) = ☐
[a] 24 [b] 23 [c] 52

2. Half a litre of juice costs 50c. How much for 2 litres?
[a] €4 [b] €2 [c] €1

3. There are ☐ days in August.
[a] 29 [b] 30 [c] 31

4. 204, 203, 202, 201, 200, ☐
[a] 201 [b] 199 [c] 99

5.  What time will it be in two hours? [a] $\frac{1}{4}$ to 4 [b] $\frac{1}{4}$ past 4 [c] $\frac{1}{4}$ to 3

6. Add the even numbers from 1 to 10. [a] 30 [b] 22 [c] 16

7. €2 − (50c + 20c + 10c) = ☐
[a] €2·80 [b] €2·20 [c] €1·20

8. 187, 188, 189, ☐ [a] 190 [b] 191 [c] 192

9. How many $\frac{1}{4}$ l cartons of juice are needed to fill a 2 l bottle?
[a] 4 [b] 8 [c] 2

10. A tennis ball is in the shape of a ____. [a] cone [b] sphere [c] circle

😞 ☐ 😐 ☐ 🙂 ☐ Score ◯ 10

Work it out

WEEK 25

1. ☐ ml = 1 l   a 100   b 1000   c 10

2. ☐ is ¼ of 16.   a 64   b 4   c 8

3. The difference between €1·20 and 50c is ☐.
   a 50c   b €1·70   c 70c

4. Which has the smallest area?
   a stamp   b envelope   c book

5. How much for five 6c lollipops?
   a 25c   b 30c   c 20c

6. Which of these is a right angle?

   a   b   c

7. 4 + 4 + 4 + 4 + 4 = ☐
   a 16   b 20   c 24

8. 6, 9, 12, 15, ☐
   a 17   b 18   c 19

9. There are ☐ hours in one day.
   a 6   b 12   c 24

10. Which is the odd one out?
   a cone   b cylinder   c square

 Score 10

WEEK 26

1. How many hours in two days?
   a 12   b 24   c 48

2. A door is measured using a ___.
   a ruler   b metre stick
   c trundle wheel

3. Three cats and five dogs have ☐ legs altogether.
   a 23   b 34   c 32

4. ¼ l of cream costs €1. How much for 2 l?   a €4   b €8   c €2

5. Salma buys cards for €1·50, a pencil for 15c and a rubber for 10c. How much change will she get from €2?   a 25c   b 35c   c 15c

6. How many lines of symmetry has a rectangle?   a 1   b 2   c 4

7. ¼ of ☐ is 10.   a 2   b 40   c 20

8. Sam is 12 years older than Paul. If Sam is 14, how old is Paul?
   a 16   b 26   c 2

9. Which of these shapes has only two faces?
   a cube   b cone   c cylinder

10. €2 − 55c = ☐   a 45c   b €1·55   c €1·45

 Score 10

Work it out

FRIDAY TESTS

WEEK 27

1. At 6:30 it is _____ 6.

    [a] $\frac{1}{2}$ past   [b] $\frac{1}{4}$ past   [c] $\frac{1}{4}$ to

2. Estimate the length of this line.

    _____

    It is closest to:

    [a] 3 cm   [b] 5 cm   [c] 9 cm

3. $\frac{1}{4}$ of 20 is ☐.   [a] 5 [b] 4 [c] 10

4. Which shape can roll and slide but cannot stack?

    [a] cylinder [b] cone [c] sphere

5. A bath can hold about ☐ litres of water. [a] 5 [b] 20 [c] 60

6. Write 1c in euro.

    [a] €1 [b] €0·10 [c] €0·01

7. $\frac{1}{2}$ of 20 ☐ $\frac{1}{4}$ of 40 [a] < [b] > [c] =

8. It is 6:00. In three hours it will be

    __:__. [a] 9:00 [b] 10:00 [c] 3:00

9. Ian is six years younger than Alex. Ian is five. How old is Alex?

    [a] 11 [b] 1 [c] 10

10. What number is missing?

    197, 198, 199, ☐

    [a] 200 [b] 300 [c] 100

 Score   10

WEEK 28

1. Jenna is six years older than Claire. Claire is ten. What age will Jenna be on her next birthday? [a] 16 [b] 4 [c] 17

2. 90 − 45 = ☐ [a] 135 [b] 55 [c] 45

3. How much?

    [a] €1·27 [b] €1·37

    [c] €0·47

4. $\frac{1}{4}$ of ☐ is 20. [a] 5 [b] 80 [c] 10

5. I am the most commonly seen 3D shape.

    [a] cuboid [b] cone [c] sphere

6. 1 kg + $\frac{1}{2}$ kg = ☐ kg [a] $\frac{1}{2}$ [b] $\frac{1}{4}$ [c] $1\frac{1}{2}$

7. This jug contains ☐ l.

    [a] $\frac{1}{4}$ [b] $\frac{1}{2}$ [c] 1

8. This shape has ☐ lines of symmetry.

    [a] 2 [b] 3 [c] 6

9. What five coins = €1·76?

    [a] €1, 50c, 10c, 10c, 5c

    [b] €1, 50c, 20c, 5c, 1c

    [c] €1, 20c, 10c, 5c, 1c

10. **08:30** shows _____. [a] $\frac{1}{2}$ past 8

    [b] $\frac{1}{4}$ past 8 [c] 8 minutes past 30

 Score   10

Work it out

FRIDAY TESTS

WEEK 29

I. What is the value of 7 in 762?

  [a] 7 [b] 70 [c] 700

2. Which has the smallest area?
  [a] your maths copy
  [b] your maths book [c] your desk

3. $10 + \boxed{} = 13 + 9$ [a] 22 [b] 12 [c] 32

4. There are 17 boys in a class of 32 children. How many girls are there? [a] 15 [b] 49 [c] 16

5. Six dogs have three bones each. How many bones are there altogether? [a] 12 [b] 18 [c] 9

6. $4 + 19 \boxed{} 30 - 8$ [a] < [b] > [c] =

7. $5 + 5 + 5 + 5 + 5 = \boxed{}$
  [a] 5 [b] 20 [c] 25

8. This flower has $\boxed{}$ lines of symmetry.
  [a] 1 [b] 2 [c] 4

9. How many petals have four flowers?
  [a] 4 [b] 12 [c] 16

10. Thirty-six children get on a bus. Twenty-five sit down. How many stay standing?
  [a] 9 [b] 10 [c] 11

☹ ☐ 😐 ☐ ☺ ☐ Score ◯ 10

WEEK 30

I. $= \boxed{}$

  [a] 83 [b] 73 [c] 93

2. School begins at around $\boxed{} : \boxed{}$.
  [a] 9:00 [b] 8:00 [c] 10:00

3. This shape is divided into $\boxed{}$s. [a] $\frac{1}{2}$ [b] $\frac{1}{4}$ [c] $\frac{1}{3}$

4. $42 - 20 = \boxed{}$ [a] 12 [b] 18 [c] 22

5. Which one is not symmetrical?
  [a] butterfly [b] hand [c] star

6. How many $\frac{1}{4}$ litres in $1\frac{1}{2}$ litres?
  [a] 4 [b] 5 [c] 6

7. $(€2·00 - 60c) - 50c = \boxed{}$
  [a] €1·10 [b] 80c [c] 90c

8. $\frac{1}{2}$ of 60 = $\boxed{}$ [a] 120 [b] 20 [c] 30

9. This is the $\boxed{}$ child.
  [a] 1st [b] 2nd [c] 6th

10. What number is missing?
  197, 198, 199, $\boxed{}$
  [a] 100 [b] 190 [c] 200

☹ ☐ 😐 ☐ ☺ ☐ Score ◯ 10

Work it out